25

BRIDGE MYTHS

EXPOSED

MASTER POINT PRESS • TORONTO

Master Point Press

331 Douglas Ave.

Toronto, Ontario Canada

M5M 1H2

(416) 781-0351 Fax (416) 781-1831

Internet www.masterpointpress.com

Canadian Cataloguing in Publication Data

Bird, David

25 bridge myths exposed / David Bird.

ISBN 1-894154-52-5

1. Contract bridge — I. Title.II Title: Twenty-five bridge myths exposed.
GV1282.3.B593 2002 795.41'5   C2002-901835-8

Editor	Ray Lee
Cover and interior design	Olena S. Sullivan
Interior format and copyediting	Deanna Bourassa

Printed and bound in Canada by Webcom Canada Ltd.

1 2 3 4 5 6 7   06 05 04 03 02

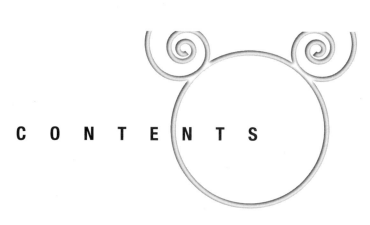

LYNNE —

MORE FOOD FOR YOUR

OBSESSION.

HAPPY VALENTINE'S DAY.

[signature]

— 04 —

C O N T E N T S

PUBLISHER'S NOTE

The quotes which begin each chapter in this book are taken from *Advanced Bridge* by Joseph Bowne Elwell, the 'Wizard of Whist', who was the leading authority on bridge-whist and auction bridge in the early twentieth century. His pupil and partner, Harold S. Vanderbilt, was eventually to invent contract bridge as we know it today. Elwell was well-known as the author of a number of popular books on bridge and whist, although it is now believed that his wife Helen (who was probably the stronger player of the two) may well have been the actual writer.

Elwell also became notorious as the victim, in 1920, of a famous unsolved murder mystery, a case which has been the basis of a number of books, both fact and fiction (*The Benson Murder Case*, by S.S. van Dine, is perhaps the best-known).

Reading Elwell's advice, one is struck by two things: first, how long many Bridge Myths have been in existence, and second, how even a century ago, expert players recognized these guidelines for what they are — simply guidelines, and not inflexible rules. A final quote from the great man sums it up:

'Certain rules, that govern the technicalities, are absolute, as they are in any game of cards, but rules in general are not the masters of bridge; rather they should be considered as second to circumstance and the fall of the cards. Brilliant plays are made in contravention of the rules...' J.B. Elwell

INTRODUCTION

Do you remember the first few times you ever played bridge? The cards in the dummy looked like thirteen random numbers and you had little idea of how to play a contract, even less of how to defend. To get you started, some friend probably gave you a few helpful hints. "You must always cover an honor with an honor, partner. He would have gone down then!" There are many such general guidelines — some of them valuable, some not. We refer to them as Bridge Myths, because every one has several exceptions and none should be followed blindly. The advice always to cover an honor with an honor, for example, is very ill-conceived. Countless tricks are lost by those who misguidedly follow this rule.

In the book we will look closely at twenty-five different Bridge Myths, covering both dummy play and defense and in not a single case are they universally true. We will look briefly at the rationale behind each guideline and then see several situations where you should ignore it. Each chapter ends with a Summary, followed by a Quiz to see if you have absorbed the material.

It was great fun writing this book and I hope you will enjoy reading it. Even if you find the book rather hard work, at least you can enjoy winning more often when you return to that greatest of sporting venues — the bridge table!

CHAPTER 1

DRAW TRUMPS STRAIGHT AWAY

 A knowledge of trump management – to know when and when not to lead trumps – is no small part of declarer's requirements.
J.B. Elwell

What is one of the greatest horrors you face, as a newcomer to the game? That one of your winners will be ruffed by a defender! Such is the fear of this ignominy that beginners tend to draw all the enemy trumps straight away, even before making a plan.

The best advice is: draw trumps straight away unless there is a good reason for not doing so. Let's remind ourselves first why it is generally right to draw trumps as soon as possible. Look at this deal:

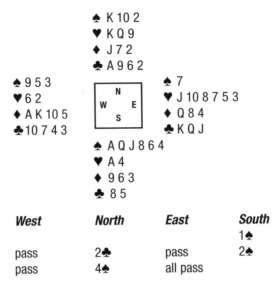

♠ K 10 2
♥ K Q 9
♦ J 7 2
♣ A 9 6 2

♠ 9 5 3
♥ 6 2
♦ A K 10 5
♣ 10 7 4 3

♠ 7
♥ J 10 8 7 5 3
♦ Q 8 4
♣ K Q J

♠ A Q J 8 6 4
♥ A 4
♦ 9 6 3
♣ 8 5

West	North	East	South
			1♠
pass	2♣	pass	2♠
pass	4♠	all pass	

You arrive in 4♠ and the defenders take the ace, king and queen of diamonds. East then switches to the club king, won with the ace in dummy. What should you do next?

You cannot afford to lose another trick. Suppose you try to dispose of your club loser before drawing trumps. You play the ace of hearts and continue with the king and queen of hearts, throwing your club loser. Disaster! West will ruff the third round of hearts, putting you one down.

Even a beginner would probably make that contract. With the maxim 'always draw trumps immediately' fresh in mind, he would play three rounds of trumps before seeking the discard. West would not then be able to ruff the third heart and the game would be made.

That was easy, then, and reminded us of the general reason why you should usually draw trumps straight away. Not so simple are the many deals where you must turn a blind eye to this guideline. Let's look at some now.

Drawing trumps would prevent you from taking a ruff

The most common reason for not drawing trumps immediately is that you need to take one or more ruffs in the dummy. That is the case here:

```
                    ♠ Q 2
                    ♥ Q 4
                    ♦ K 9 7 5 2
                    ♣ 10 9 6 2
   ♠ 8 4 3                        ♠ 6 5
   ♥ J 9 8 5        N             ♥ 10 6 3
   ♦ J 8 3      W       E         ♦ A Q 10 6
   ♣ K Q 3          S             ♣ A J 7 4
                    ♠ A K J 10 9 7
                    ♥ A K 7 2
                    ♦ 4
                    ♣ 8 5
```

West	North	East	South
			1♠
pass	1NT	pass	2♥
pass	2♠	pass	4♠
all pass			

West leads the ♣K against your spade game and continues with queen and another club to his partner's jack. You ruff the third round of clubs in your hand. What now?

Suppose you draw trumps straight away. Since you have only nine tricks you may decide to play a diamond towards the king next. This does not work. East wins with the ace and you will make only nine tricks.

Before embarking on any contract you should make a plan. Here you can see three certain losers in the minors and must seek to dispose of another possible loser — the fourth heart. As we have seen, you need some luck to achieve a discard on the ♦K. A better plan is to ruff a heart in dummy. After ruffing the third round of clubs, you should cash the queen and ace of hearts. You then ruff your remaining low heart with the queen of trumps. You take the ruff with a master trump just in case East started with only two hearts and would otherwise be able to overruff. You can then draw trumps and score your tenth trick with the ♥K.

Drawing trumps would waste an important entry to dummy

Sometimes you need to use dummy's trump suit as a means of gaining access to a long side suit there. In that case you must delay drawing trumps until the side suit is ready to run. Look at this deal:

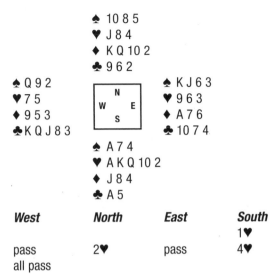

```
                    ♠ 10 8 5
                    ♥ J 8 4
                    ♦ K Q 10 2
                    ♣ 9 6 2
     ♠ Q 9 2          ┌─────────┐       ♠ K J 6 3
     ♥ 7 5            │    N    │       ♥ 9 6 3
     ♦ 9 5 3          │  W   E  │       ♦ A 7 6
     ♣ K Q J 8 3      │    S    │       ♣ 10 7 4
                      └─────────┘
                    ♠ A 7 4
                    ♥ A K Q 10 2
                    ♦ J 8 4
                    ♣ A 5
```

West	North	East	South
			1♥
pass	2♥	pass	4♥
all pass			

West leads the ♣K and you win immediately since a spade switch would be unwelcome. What will happen if you draw three rounds of trumps now? When you turn to the diamond suit, East will hold up the ace for two rounds. You will then have no entry to the good diamond in dummy. You will lose two spades, one diamond and one club. One down!

To enjoy the long diamond you must leave the jack of trumps in dummy, as an entry. So, win the first club and draw two rounds of trumps with the ace and king. You must now risk playing on diamonds, even though there is still a trump out. As the cards lie, the defenders cannot score a diamond ruff. Let's assume that East holds up his diamond ace until the third round. When you regain the lead you will cross to the jack of trumps, drawing the defenders' last trump. You can then throw one of your spade losers on the good diamond in dummy.

Drawing trumps would allow the defenders to cash a trick

Another common situation where it is wrong to play on trumps straight away is when the opponents will gain the lead and will be able to cash a setting trick. Take the South cards on this deal:

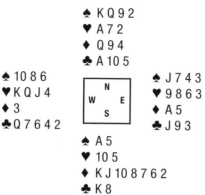

```
            ♠ K Q 9 2
            ♥ A 7 2
            ♦ Q 9 4
            ♣ A 10 5
♠ 10 8 6              ♠ J 7 4 3
♥ K Q J 4            ♥ 9 8 6 3
♦ 3                  ♦ A 5
♣ Q 7 6 4 2         ♣ J 9 3
            ♠ A 5
            ♥ 10 5
            ♦ K J 10 8 7 6 2
            ♣ K 8
```

You reach a small slam in diamonds and West leads the ♥K, won with dummy's ace. You can see what will happen if you play trumps straight away. East will win and the defenders will score a heart trick to put you one down. Before playing trumps you must dispose of your heart loser. You can do this by playing three rounds of spades. The defenders both follow all the way and you discard the last heart from your hand. Only then is it safe to play trumps.

On the next deal the opening lead has not yet set up a defensive trick but you must prepare your discard before you tackle the trump suit:

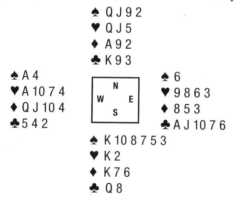

```
            ♠ Q J 9 2
            ♥ Q J 5
            ♦ A 9 2
            ♣ K 9 3
♠ A 4                ♠ 6
♥ A 10 7 4          ♥ 9 8 6 3
♦ Q J 10 4          ♦ 8 5 3
♣ 5 4 2             ♣ A J 10 7 6
            ♠ K 10 8 7 5 3
            ♥ K 2
            ♦ K 7 6
            ♣ Q 8
```

You bid to the spade game and the ♦Q is led. Suppose you win the trick and play a trump immediately. When West takes the trump ace, he will play another diamond and establish a trick in the suit. There is no way to avoid a diamond loser and you will go one down, losing one trick in every suit.

The highest priority, after winning the diamond lead, is to establish a discard for your potential diamond loser. You should therefore play on hearts, forcing out the ace. When you win the second round of diamonds you can discard your diamond loser on the third round of hearts. Only then will it be time to draw trumps.

Does anything else occur to you on that last deal? If West ducks the first heart and wins the second, then knocks out your second high diamond, you will need a quick entry to dummy in order to take a discard. You must therefore win the opening lead in your own hand, with your diamond king. The ace of diamonds will then serve as an entry to the established heart in the dummy.

Summary

✓ It is usually best to draw trumps straight away unless there is a reason for not doing so.

✓ Do not draw trumps immediately if this would exhaust dummy's trumps and you need them to take a ruff or two.

✓ Do not draw trumps immediately when this would remove a high trump in dummy that you need as an entry.

✓ Do not draw trumps straight away if this would allow the defenders to score or establish a setting trick. Look for a way to discard your potential loser, or to set up a discard for it.

DRAW TRUMPS STRAIGHT AWAY

NOW TRY THESE...

1)
```
              ♠ Q 4
              ♥ A 8 3
              ♦ K Q 4
              ♣ 10 8 7 5 2
```
♣Q led

```
              ♠ K 9 5
              ♥ K Q J 10 7 2
              ♦ A 10 3
              ♣ A
```

You bid to 6♥ and West leads the ♣Q to your ace. Will you draw trumps straight away? If not, why not?

2)
```
              ♠ A 4
              ♥ A 8 3
              ♦ J 8 2
              ♣ A 9 7 4 3
```
♥J led

```
              ♠ K Q J 10 9 5
              ♥ K 4
              ♦ A 7 3
              ♣ K 2
```

You arrive in 6♠ and West leads the ♥J. How will you play the hand? Will you draw trumps straight away? If not, why not?

3)
```
              ♠ K 9 5
              ♥ Q J 8 5
              ♦ Q 10 4
              ♣ K 8 5
```
♣Q led

```
              ♠ 4
              ♥ K 10 9 6 3
              ♦ K J 9 6
              ♣ A 6 4
```

West leads the ♣Q against your heart game. Will you draw trumps straight away? If not, why not?

ANSWERS

1) To bring your total to twelve tricks you will need a spade ruff in the dummy. Suppose you draw two rounds of trumps and find that they break 3-1. When you knock out the ace of spades the defender who wins may be able to play a third round of trumps, depriving you of your ruff. One down! To prevent this from happening, you should play on spades at Trick 2, forcing out the ace. When you regain the lead you will draw two rounds of trumps with the king-queen and take a spade ruff with the ace.

2) You have only eleven certain tricks and must set up at least one club trick to make the slam. Suppose you win the opening heart lead with the king and draw trumps. With only one side entry to dummy remaining (the ♥A), you will then need clubs to break 3-3. If instead you retain the trump ace as an extra entry, you can succeed against a 4-2 club break. Win with the ♥K and play the king and ace of clubs. Ruff a club with the king and draw two rounds of trumps with the queen and ace. If clubs broke 4-2 you can now ruff another club with the jack, and proceed to draw trumps. The established club will give you the slam and you still have the ♥A in dummy to reach it.

3) If you win the club lead and play trumps immediately, the defenders will win and set up their club trick. You will then go one down, suffering a loser in every suit. You need to set up a discard for your club loser. However, it is no good knocking out the ♦A because you would not be able to take a discard on the fourth diamond until trumps had been drawn. The only chance is to win the club lead with the ace and lead a spade towards dummy's king. If West holds the ♠A, you will set up a quick discard for your club loser.

HOLD UP AN ACE

Holding up is a strategy whose idea is to retain a high card until one hand is exhausted and cannot lead the suit to the opposite hand. *J.B. Elwell*

You reach 3NT and the opponents attack in their best suit, where you hold ace third. Very early in their bridge careers, beginners are told that they must **always hold up an ace**. What is the point of doing this? It is to break the communications between the defenders, so that they cannot enjoy the long cards in the suit. Let's see a typical deal where it is good play to hold up an ace.

```
                    ♠ 10 3
                    ♥ K J 2
                    ♦ K J 7 2
                    ♣ A 9 6 2
      ♠ K Q J 9 5                      ♠ 8 6 4
      ♥ 9 6 4         N                ♥ 10 8 7 3
      ♦ 9 5       W       E            ♦ Q 8 4
      ♣ Q J 3         S                ♣ 10 7 4
                    ♠ A 7 2
                    ♥ A Q 5
                    ♦ A 10 6 3
                    ♣ K 8 5
```

Partner raises your 1NT opening to 3NT and West leads the king of spades. You can count eight top tricks and need one more to make your game. If you win the first or second round of spades the defenders' communications are intact (East still has a spade). You will therefore need to score a ninth trick without letting either defender on lead. It is no good playing for a 3-3 break in clubs because you would lose one club and four spades. Instead you will have to guess which defender holds the ♦Q.

Good players hate having to guess to make a contract. There is absolutely no need to guess on this deal! You should hold up the ace of spades until the third round. You then play the ace of diamonds and a diamond to dummy's jack. Even though this loses, you will still make 3NT. Thanks to your hold-up East has no spade to play. (If he did have a spade left, the suit would have broken 4-4 and pose no threat.) You will make one spade, three hearts, three diamonds and two clubs — a total of nine.

After your hold-up East became the 'safe hand'. Since you could afford to have him gain the lead, you took the diamond finesse 'into the safe hand'.

The time has come to look at some situations when it would not be a good idea to hold up an ace.

Holding up an ace would allow a dangerous switch

Sometimes a continuation of the suit that has been led is not the biggest threat to your contract. If you hold up the ace of that suit the defenders may switch elsewhere, setting up enough tricks to beat you. That is the case here:

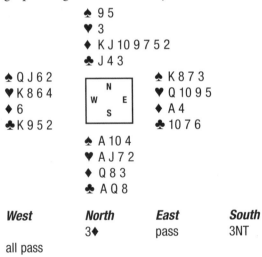

	♠ 9 5
	♥ 3
	♦ K J 10 9 7 5 2
	♣ J 4 3

♠ Q J 6 2   ♠ K 8 7 3
♥ K 8 6 4   ♥ Q 10 9 5
♦ 6   ♦ A 4
♣ K 9 5 2   ♣ 10 7 6

	♠ A 10 4
	♥ A J 7 2
	♦ Q 8 3
	♣ A Q 8

West	North	East	South
	3♦	pass	3NT
all pass			

Playing fourth-best leads, West starts with the ♠2 against your 3NT. How should you play when East contributes the king?

Let's think what may happen if you hold up the ♠A. East knows from his partner's ♠2 lead that he holds only four spades. You surely have a spade stopper for your 3NT bid, so a spade return from East is likely to net only three spades and the diamond ace — not enough to beat the game. East may well switch to the ♥10. This is not good news for you. If you rise with the ♥A immediately and play on diamonds you will lose one spade, three hearts and the ♦A. If instead you duck the heart, or cover with the jack, the defenders can beat you by playing either major.

Now let's consider what will happen if you win the first round of spades and play on diamonds. You will make the contract! You too know from the ♠2 lead that West holds only four spades. The defenders will therefore be able to score just three spades and the diamond ace.

On the next deal you cannot be certain that the suit led by the opponents is breaking 4-4. What you do know is that East will make a very damaging play if you leave him on lead at Trick 2.

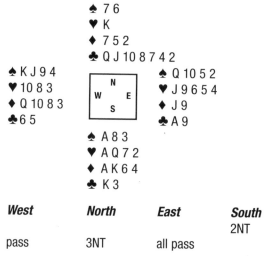

	♠ 7 6		
	♥ K		
	♦ 7 5 2		
	♣ Q J 10 8 7 4 2		

♠ K J 9 4   ♠ Q 10 5 2
♥ 10 8 3   ♥ J 9 6 5 4
♦ Q 10 8 3   ♦ J 9
♣ 6 5   ♣ A 9

♠ A 8 3
♥ A Q 7 2
♦ A K 6 4
♣ K 3

West	North	East	South
			2NT
pass	3NT	all pass	

West leads the ♠4 against 3NT, East playing the queen. On many similar deals it would be right to hold up the spade ace. When spades were 5-3, you would then make the contract when the ace of clubs lay with the three-card spade holding. What will happen if you hold up the ace of spades on this deal? East will surely seize his chance to kill dummy's club suit by switching to a heart, removing the only side entry to the dummy. When you play on clubs, he will hold up the ace until the second round and the dummy will then be useless to you. Even if the diamond suit breaks 3-3, allowing you to set up an extra trick there, you cannot bump your total to more than eight tricks.

So, even though it is entirely possible West holds five spades to his partner's three, you should take what is your only practical chance of making the contract by winning the first spade. You continue with the king of clubs, ducked, and a second round of clubs. When the spade suit does prove to be 4-4, you make the game. If the spades had been 5-3, you were not destined to make the contract.

Holding up an ace kills a second stopper

When you hold a stopper of A-J-x in the suit that has been led, you must consider your play carefully. If the defender on your right is likely to gain the lead later, you should normally hold up the ace for two rounds, playing as if you held only A-x-x. If instead the defender on your left is likely to gain the lead, you do best to win the ace immediately. Your remaining J-x will then act as a second stopper.

This deal illustrates the situation:

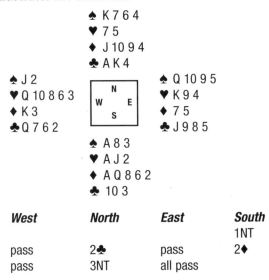

West	North	East	South
			1NT
pass	2♣	pass	2♦
pass	3NT	all pass	

West leads the ♥6 against 3NT, East playing the king. Before deciding whether to hold up, you must consider your play of the contract as a whole. You have six top tricks and can score three more from the diamond suit, even if the finesse loses. Since West may gain the lead when you play on diamonds but East cannot, you should win East's king of hearts with the ace. You cross to a club and take a diamond finesse, which loses. That causes no problem, because with West on lead your ♥J-2 stops the suit. If West switches elsewhere, you will score the nine tricks you need. If he persists with hearts, you will make an overtrick.

Look back at the diagram and imagine that the ace-queen of diamonds were in dummy, the jack-ten-nine in your hand. You would then allow East's king of hearts to win the first trick. You would hold up the heart ace on the second round too, winning on the third round. When you took a losing finesse into the East hand, all would again be well. East would have no heart to return.

Holding up an ace would prevent a throw-in

When you hold ace third in the suit led, it is sometimes best to win the second round of the suit, planning to put a defender on lead later — with a third round. He may then have to give you a trick after cashing his winners.

Take the South cards on this deal:

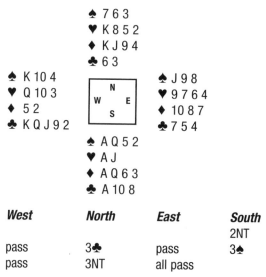

```
                  ♠ 7 6 3
                  ♥ K 8 5 2
                  ♦ K J 9 4
                  ♣ 6 3
  ♠ K 10 4                        ♠ J 9 8
  ♥ Q 10 3         N              ♥ 9 7 6 4
  ♦ 5 2         W     E           ♦ 10 8 7
  ♣ K Q J 9 2      S              ♣ 7 5 4
                  ♠ A Q 5 2
                  ♥ A J
                  ♦ A Q 6 3
                  ♣ A 10 8
```

West	North	East	South
			2NT
pass	3♣	pass	3♠
pass	3NT	all pass	

West leads the ♣K against your contract of 3NT. Suppose first that you hold up the ♣A for two rounds, to exhaust East of the suit. It doesn't help you much, does it? There is no way of creating an extra trick that involves East gaining the lead. That's because both the major-suit finesses will be into the danger hand (West). Can you see anything better?

The first step in planning any notrump contract is to count your top tricks. Here you have eight top tricks and therefore need one more. You could rely on luck, taking one or the other of major-suit finesses. A better idea is to win the second round of clubs, play three rounds of diamonds (to remove West's safe exit in that suit) and then throw West on lead with a third round of clubs. He can cash two more clubs but this does not embarrass you for discards. You throw two spades and a heart from dummy, two spades from your own hand. These cards will remain:

```
                  ♠ 7
                  ♥ K 8 5
                  ♦ J
                  ♣ —
  ♠ K 10                          ♠ J 9 8
  ♥ Q 10 3         N              ♥ 9 7
  ♦ —           W     E           ♦ —
  ♣ —              S              ♣ —
                  ♠ A Q
                  ♥ A J
                  ♦ 3
                  ♣ —
```

West must now give you an extra trick by leading into one of your tenaces. Whether he plays a spade or a heart you will have a ninth trick.

Summary

✓ The purpose of holding up an ace is to cut the communication between the defenders. You do this by exhausting one defender of the suit that has been led. He then becomes the 'safe hand' and you can develop tricks safely if you take care to lose the lead only to him.

✓ Do not hold up an ace when a switch to another suit is dangerous and you may be able to make the contract without a hold-up.

✓ When you hold ace third in the suit that has been led, you can sometimes execute a throw-in by winning the second round and later exiting in that suit.

HOLD UP AN ACE

1)

    ♠ 8 6
    ♥ 9 4
    ♦ K J 4
    ♣ A J 10 8 7 4

```
      N
  W       E
      S
```

    ♠ A 9 5
    ♥ K 7 3 2
    ♦ A Q 3
    ♣ Q 9 3

West	North	East	South
			1NT
pass	3NT	all pass	

West leads a fourth-best ♠3 to his partner's queen. Will you hold up the spade ace? What is the reason for your choice?

2)

    ♠ A 6
    ♥ A J 10 3
    ♦ Q J 10 8 3
    ♣ 7 4

```
      N
  W       E
      S
```

    ♠ K Q J 5
    ♥ Q 4
    ♦ A 9 7 4
    ♣ A 9 2

West	North	East	South
			1NT
pass	2♣	pass	2♠
pass	3NT	all pass	

West leads the ♣K against 3NT. Will you hold up the ace? What is the reason for your choice? Whether or not you decide to win the first club, how will you play the contract?

ANSWERS

1) You should not hold up the ace. Let's consider first what will happen if you take the spade ace immediately. You will make ten tricks if West holds the ♣K and you will go down if East holds that card. So, that gives you a 50% chance of success. What will happen if you hold up the spade ace? First of all, East may switch to hearts and the defenders could take four heart tricks, beating the contract even when the ♣K was onside. Secondly, the hold-up is never likely to gain. If East holds the ♣K and the ♥A he will see that it is futile to persevere with spades after your hold-up. (That will give the defenders only two spades, the ♥A and the ♣K.) He will therefore switch to hearts at Trick 2, setting up at least three heart tricks to go with the two black-suit winners. Hold up the spade ace and your prospects, against sensible defense, are very poor indeed. Better to grab the solid 50% chance!

2) You have seven top tricks and need to develop two more. Suppose you win the first or second club. The defenders' communications will still be intact in the dangerous case where the clubs are divided 5-3. You will therefore have to guess which red-suit finesse to take. A better idea is to hold up the ace of clubs for two rounds. East is now the 'safe hand' (either he has no clubs left or the suit started 4-4 and poses no threat). You must look for a safe way to develop your extra tricks. A diamond finesse would be 'into the danger hand'. If it failed you would go down. A better idea is to run the ♥Q. You don't mind if that finesse loses because it will be the safe hand that gains the lead. You set up an eighth and ninth trick for yourself and will lose at most three clubs and a heart.

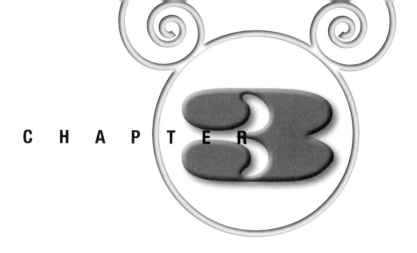

C H A P T E R 3

WIN AS CHEAPLY AS POSSIBLE

 Use proper judgement in ridding yourself of cards that you fear may block a suit. *J.B. Elwell*

When you are last to play to a trick it is fairly obvious that you should normally win with the lowest card possible. By doing so, you retain the higher cards for later in the play.

♥ 8 6 2

♥ K Q 7 3   ♥ 10 5 4

♥ A J 9

West leads the ♥3 against your no-trump contract, East playing the ten. Obviously, you win with the jack rather than the ace, ensuring that you will score two tricks from the suit. Let's look straight away at some situations where it is not a good idea to win as cheaply as possible.

Winning with the cheapest card gives away information

When you have two touching honors as declarer — K-Q, for example — do you think it can possibly matter which honor you use to win the trick? Many bridge players go through their entire lifetime winning with the cheaper card (the queen from king-queen) and thinking nothing of it. This is nearly always wrong! Why is that? Because you give valuable information to the defenders.

Suppose West leads the ♥6 against 3NT and this is the lie of the suit:

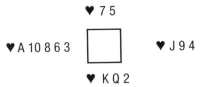

If you win East's jack with the queen you are letting West know that you also hold the king. (If East held the king he would have played it.) If West gains the lead later in the play he will have no temptation whatsoever to lead another low heart, in the hope that East holds the missing king. Instead he will seek an entry to his partner's hand in another suit, so a second round of hearts can be led through your king.

Any good declarer will capture the jack with the king, rather than the queen. Do you see how much more difficult it is for West now? His partner might have started with Q-J-4 and played the lower of touching cards, his jack forcing declarer's king. When West regains the lead now, he will have to guess who has the ♥Q.

It's worth looking at a full deal that illustrates this theme:

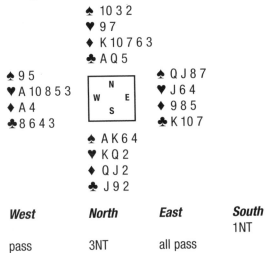

West	North	East	South
			1NT
pass	3NT	all pass	

West leads the ♥5 against 3NT. You try dummy's nine and East covers with the jack. How should you play the contract?

Let's see first what will happen if you win with the queen, rather than the king. When you play on diamonds West will win with the ace. Knowing that you hold the king of hearts, because East did not play it at Trick 1, West will not be tempted to play another heart. Whatever else he does, you will go down. You have only eight tricks and when East gains the lead he will play a second round of hearts through your king.

Look next at the problem you cause West by winning East's jack of hearts with the king at Trick 1. When West gains the lead with the ace of diamonds, it will seem all too possible to him that you have nine or ten tricks ready to run. (Suppose you held the king of clubs instead of the queen of hearts, for example.) West may well continue hearts in the hope that his partner holds the queen. This will give you a ninth trick and you will make your game.

Perhaps you are saying to yourself: 'West might switch to a black suit anyway.' He might, it's true. But you have made life difficult for him. You have put him to a guess. Every time you make the defenders guess in this way you are giving yourself an extra chance. A fair proportion of the time they will guess wrong.

Here is another example of this very important idea:

West leads the ♠4 and East plays the ten. You should win with the queen, not the jack. If West gains the lead subsequently, he may be tempted to continue the suit in the hope that his partner holds the ♠J. If instead you make the mistake of winning with the jack, the cheaper card, West can place you with the A-Q-J and will not continue the suit.

The same idea applies if you are playing on this spade suit yourself. You should play low to the queen, rather than low to the jack. By doing so you give away less information. Playing the correct card from equals is much more important than you may think.

Winning with a high card for deceptive purposes

Even when your high cards are not touching, there can be some advantage to winning with a higher card than is necessary. One common reason is that you want to feign weakness in the suit that the defenders have led against notrump. By doing so, you hope to tempt a continuation in the suit, rather than a switch to your unprotected suit.

Take the South cards and look for such a move on this deal:

```
              ♠ 10 3
              ♥ 9 4
              ♦ Q J 7 4 2
              ♣ A Q 6 2
♠ K Q 6 5      ┌─────────┐      ♠ A 9 8 4
♥ K 10 8 6 2   │    N    │      ♥ J 7 3
♦ K 5          │  W   E  │      ♦ 9 8
♣ 9 3          │    S    │      ♣ 10 8 7 4
              └─────────┘
              ♠ J 7 2
              ♥ A Q 5
              ♦ A 10 6 3
              ♣ K J 5
```

West	North	East	South
			1NT
pass	3NT	all pass	

West leads the ♥6 to his partner's jack. Let's see first what is likely to happen if you make the seemingly obvious move of winning with the queen. You cross to dummy with a club and run the queen of diamonds. When West wins with the king he can see that a heart continuation is futile, since you will surely score at least four diamonds, three clubs and two hearts. There is every chance that West will switch to spades and the resultant four spade tricks for the defense will beat the contract.

Let's go back to the first trick and make life much more difficult for West. Win East's ♥J with the ace! When you cross to dummy and take a losing diamond finesse West will surely continue hearts, placing his partner with Q-J-x in the suit. Your ♥Q will win the trick and you will have a good story to tell in the bar afterwards... and for the next few weeks.

BY THE WAY

This deception is possible only when East holds the jack and therefore a possible Q-J-x. If instead West held K-J-x-x-x and East held 10-x-x, it would be pointless to win with the ace. West would know from East's failure to play the queen that you must hold that card.

Winning with a high card to create an entry to dummy

There is another important situation where it will pay you to win with an unnecessarily high card — when you hope to create an extra entry to the dummy. Take the South cards in 3NT here:

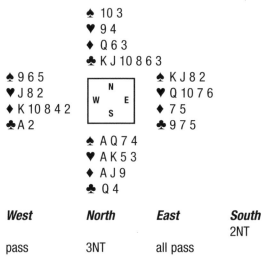

```
              ♠ 10 3
              ♥ 9 4
              ♦ Q 6 3
              ♣ K J 10 8 6 3
♠ 9 6 5                        ♠ K J 8 2
♥ J 8 2          N             ♥ Q 10 7 6
♦ K 10 8 4 2   W   E           ♦ 7 5
♣ A 2            S             ♣ 9 7 5
              ♠ A Q 7 4
              ♥ A K 5 3
              ♦ A J 9
              ♣ Q 4
```

West	North	East	South
			2NT
pass	3NT	all pass	

West leads the ♦4 to his partner's seven. Suppose you win with the nine. What next? The answer is that you will go down. West will hold up his ♣A on the first round. When he wins the second round and exits safely in a major, you will have no way to reach the four good clubs in dummy.

A better idea is to win the first trick with the ♦A, an unnecessarily high card. This brings a smile to the face of dummy's ♦Q. Sitting over West's king, with two lower cards in your own hand, the queen now represents a certain entry to dummy. You clear the clubs, West winning the second round. You can then capture West's major-suit return and lead a diamond towards dummy, establishing an entry to the club winners.

Sometimes winning with an unnecessarily high card will not only ease your access to the dummy, it will allow you to score an extra trick by taking a subsequent finesse. Look at this deal:

```
              ♠ 10 5 2
              ♥ 8 7 3
              ♦ J 9 7 6
              ♣ A J 6
♠ Q 8                          ♠ K J 9 3
♥ K J 6 4        N             ♥ Q 10
♦ 8 4          W   E           ♦ 10 5 3 2
♣ Q 10 8 5 2     S             ♣ 7 4 3
              ♠ A 7 6 4
              ♥ A 9 5 2
              ♦ A K Q
              ♣ K 9
```

West	North	East	South
			2NT
pass	3NT	all pass	

West leads the ♣5 against 3NT. You play low from the dummy and East contributes the seven. How should you play the contract?

If you win the trick cheaply, with the nine, your fate is obvious. After playing the three top diamonds in your hand, you will have to overtake the king of clubs with the ace to reach dummy and cash the fourth diamond trick. Restricted to just two club tricks, you will go one down.

Instead you should win the first trick with the king, an unnecessarily high card. You unblock the three diamond winners and finesse dummy's jack of clubs. The finesse wins, as West's low spot-card lead had given you every reason to expect, and you now make nine tricks: four diamonds, three clubs and the two major-suit aces.

Summary

✓ You should normally win a trick with the cheapest available card. You preserve the higher cards for subsequent tricks

✓ As declarer you should generally win with the higher (or highest) of touching cards. By doing so, you disguise your holding.

✓ By winning with a higher card than necessary in your hand, you may be able to create an extra entry to dummy.

WIN AS CHEAPLY AS POSSIBLE

NOW TRY THESE...

1) The defender who plays third to a trick is told to play the lower of touching cards (the jack from Q-J). Declarer is supposed to play the higher card. Why is the 'rule' different in the two cases?

2)

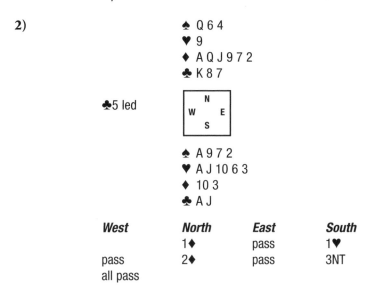

♠ Q 6 4
♥ 9
♦ A Q J 9 7 2
♣ K 8 7

♣5 led

♠ A 9 7 2
♥ A J 10 6 3
♦ 10 3
♣ A J

West	North	East	South
	1♦	pass	1♥
pass	2♦	pass	3NT
all pass			

West leads the ♣5 and East plays the ♣9. Will you win with the ace or the jack? What is the reason for your choice?

3)

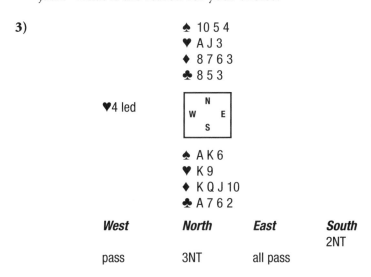

♠ 10 5 4
♥ A J 3
♦ 8 7 6 3
♣ 8 5 3

♥4 led

♠ A K 6
♥ K 9
♦ K Q J 10
♣ A 7 6 2

West	North	East	South
			2NT
pass	3NT	all pass	

West leads the ♥4, his partner playing the seven. Will you win with the king or the nine? What is the reason for your choice?

ANSWERS

1) Playing the lower of two touching cards as a defender gives your partner information about your hand. Suppose West leads the ♠4 against a suit contract and the suit lies like this:

```
              ♠ 7 6 3
♠ K 9 8 4    ┌─────┐    ♠ Q J 2
             │     │
             └─────┘
              ♠ A 10 5
```

When East's jack forces declarer's ace, West can tell that East holds the queen. (Otherwise declarer would surely have won with the queen.) If it was East's policy to play the queen from such a holding — not a good idea — West would be in the dark as to the position of the missing ♠J. He would not know if it was safe to continue the suit next time he gained the lead.

The reason why declarer does not follow the same advice is that he does not want to give information about his hand. Indeed, he should aim to disguise his holding, to make the defense more difficult.

2) You should win with the ♣A to preserve the ♣K as an entry to dummy. The ♠Q is not a certain entry because East may hold the king. Nor can you be sure of entering dummy in the diamond suit. If East holds K-x-x in diamonds he will surely duck when you take your first finesse. When he wins on the second round, you will be glad that the ♣K is available as an entry!

3) Once you have removed the ♦A you will have eight top tricks available. By far the best chance of a ninth trick is to finesse dummy's ♥J. (West is a big favorite to hold the ♥Q after his low heart lead; clubs are not any sort of favorite to break 3-3!) If you win the first round of hearts with the nine, you will not be able to take this finesse. The suit will be 'blocked'. Instead you should win the opening lead with the king. You clear the diamonds, win the black-suit return, and finesse the ♥J. If this wins, as you expect, you will have nine tricks.

C H A P T E R

PLAY LOW IN SECOND SEAT

 If you will try to infer why the defense is leading that suit, it will assist you to decide on the correct second-hand play. ***J.B. Elwell***

The well-known guideline, **play low in the second seat**, is just as valid for declarer as it is for the defenders. When your left-hand opponent has led to a trick, you should not expend a high card from the dummy without good reason. Many players go wrong in this position:

```
                      ♠ Q 9 3
      ♠ 8 2          ┌───────┐        ♠ K J 10 6 4
                     │       │
                     └───────┘
                      ♠ A 7 5
```

West leads the ♠8, a high spot-card that implies he does not hold an honor. It is pointless to play dummy's queen. The card is certain to be covered and your future in the suit will be non-existent.

If instead you play low from dummy, you have two interesting options. The first is to win with the ace, preserving dummy's Q-9 as a stopper in the suit, should East gain the lead. The second is to cover with dummy's nine and to allow East's ten to win. He cannot safely continue the suit, so your guard remains intact.

You will not be surprised to hear that there are several situations in which it is beneficial to play high from the dummy even though you could have played low and won the trick in your hand. Let's see the most important of them.

Playing high to preserve an entry

When you have the chance to win the opening lead in your own hand or the dummy, the decision will usually be based on future communications. Would you play the next deal correctly?

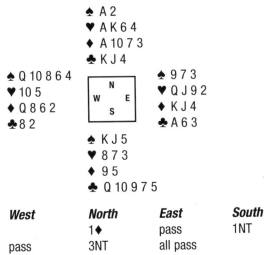

	♠ A 2	
	♥ A K 6 4	
	♦ A 10 7 3	
	♣ K J 4	

West	North	East	South
	1♦	pass	1NT
pass	3NT	all pass	

West leads the ♠6 against your contract of 3NT. How do you plan to arrive at nine tricks?

Suppose you give the matter insufficient thought, playing low from the dummy and winning East's nine with the jack. When you play on clubs East will hold up the ♣A until the third round. West, meanwhile, will start to throw away spades. This is to let East know that he should not persevere with the suit (West knows that South holds the ♠K; East does not.) The defenders will then play on hearts, followed by diamonds, setting up five tricks for themselves. You will not be able to reach the two good clubs.

What went wrong? By running the spade lead to the South hand you killed a precious entry. Win instead with dummy's ♠A and there is no problem at all. You clear the club suit and can use the ♠K as an entry to reach the long clubs. You score two spade tricks (all you need), three top cards in the red suits and four club winners.

Playing high to break the defenders' communications

You can sometimes break the defenders' communications by playing a high card from dummy. It's the sort of play that you could miss for a lifetime if you had never read about it in a book. Look at this deal:

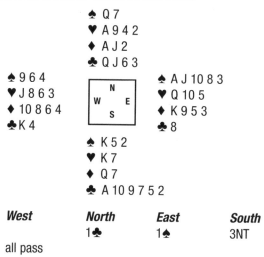

West	North	East	South
	1♣	1♠	3NT

all pass

West leads a spade against 3NT and you must aim to make nine tricks even if the club finesse is destined to fail. Any ideas?

Suppose you play the ♠7 from dummy on the first trick. East will play the ten and you will go down. If you win with the king, the defenders' spades will be ready to run when the club finesse loses. If instead you allow East's ten to win, East will return a low spade at Trick 2, retaining communications with his ace. One down, again.

Now try something more inspired on the first trick. Rise with dummy's ♠Q! East cannot let this card win or you will score two spade tricks. He has to win with the ace and now you can hold up the spade king until the third round. It will then be safe to take the club finesse. West will have no spade to play when he wins with the ♣K. By rising with the ♠Q you force East to take his ♠A at a moment that is inconvenient for him.

Playing high to avoid a ruff

A somewhat less complicated reason for playing high from the dummy is that you fear the lead is a singleton and that a ruff is imminent. Would you have read the cards correctly on this deal?

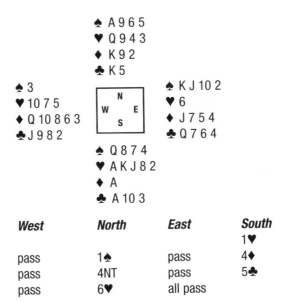

	♠ A 9 6 5		
	♥ Q 9 4 3		
	♦ K 9 2		
	♣ K 5		

♠ 3
♥ 10 7 5
♦ Q 10 8 6 3
♣ J 9 8 2

♠ K J 10 2
♥ 6
♦ J 7 5 4
♣ Q 7 6 4

♠ Q 8 7 4
♥ A K J 8 2
♦ A
♣ A 10 3

West	North	East	South
			1♥
pass	1♠	pass	4♦
pass	4NT	pass	5♣
pass	6♥	all pass	

You reach 6♥ after your 4♦ splinter bid has shown at most one diamond and initially agreed spades as trumps. West leads the ♠3. How will you play?

What is the likely lie of the spades? West knows that you and the dummy both have length in spades. It is barely possible that he would risk a lead from a holding such as K-J-x-x in the suit. You can be almost certain that the opening lead is a singleton and that East holds the ♠K. Rise with dummy's ♠A and draw trumps. One of your spades can be thrown on dummy's ♦K and you will then lead towards the spade queen to bring home the slam.

Summary

✓ The well-known defenders' rule 'play low in second seat' applies with equal force to declarer's play from the dummy when left-hand-opponent has led to the trick.

✓ When you can win the trick in either hand, consider where you may need an entry later in the play.

✓ Playing an honor from dummy can sometimes force right-hand-opponent to win his ace, breaking the defenders' communications.

PLAY LOW IN SECOND SEAT

NOW TRY THESE...

1)

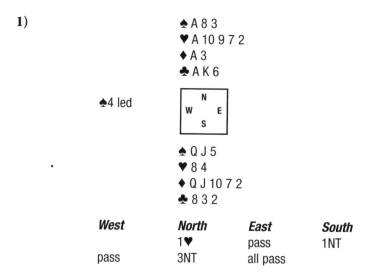

♠ A 8 3
♥ A 10 9 7 2
♦ A 3
♣ A K 6

♠4 led

♠ Q J 5
♥ 8 4
♦ Q J 10 7 2
♣ 8 3 2

West	North	East	South
	1♥	pass	1NT
pass	3NT	all pass	

West leads a fourth-best ♠4 against your contract of 3NT. How do you plan to arrive at nine tricks?

2)

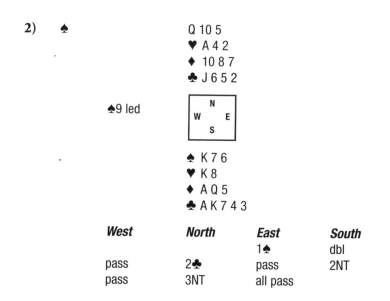

♠ Q 10 5
♥ A 4 2
♦ 10 8 7
♣ J 6 5 2

♠9 led

♠ K 7 6
♥ K 8
♦ A Q 5
♣ A K 7 4 3

West	North	East	South
		1♠	dbl
pass	2♣	pass	2NT
pass	3NT	all pass	

West leads the ♠9 against 3NT. How will you play?

ANSWERS

1) Suppose you run the opening lead to your hand, winning with the queen or jack. You can set up the diamond suit by playing ace and another diamond but you will have no entry to the cards that you establish. If West wins with the diamond king he will not play another spade. He will switch to clubs or hearts and you will go down. To make the contract you must rise with the ace of spades at Trick 1, retaining the spade Q-J as a later means of entry to your hand. You continue with ace and another diamond, setting up that suit. If West wins the diamond and switches to a low heart, you must play low from dummy (in case East holds K-Q-J-x). You win the return and play a spade to set up an entry to your hand. If instead East wins the diamond, or West wins and switches to a club, you will win the defenders' switch immediately and play on spades. The contract is guaranteed by this line of play.

2) All will be easy if the club queen falls in two rounds so you should aim to make the contract if one defender holds ♣Q-x-x — no matter which defender it is. Suppose you win the ♠9 with the king (or the ♠9 is covered by the ten, jack and king). You will go down when West turns up with a club guard and can lead a second spade through dummy's queen. Suppose instead that you duck the first round of spades, winning the second or the third in order to exhaust West of the suit. You will then go down when East has a club guard.

   To give yourself the best chance you must play the ♠Q at Trick 1! East has to win, or you will score two tricks in the suit. He cannot then safely continue the suit, since this would allow you to score both your king and dummy's ten. If East switches to a different suit you will have time to concede a club trick, if necessary. Should the club suit proide only four tricks, you will have to take the diamond finesse to bring your total to nine tricks.

C H A P T E R

EIGHT EVER, NINE NEVER

 The number of cards in the suit will often influence you in taking or not taking the finesse. *J.B. Elwell*

The ditty **eight ever, nine never** is to remind novice players whether they should finesse when missing a queen in one of these situations:

1) ♠ A J 6 2

♠ K 7 5 3

2) ♥ K J 7 4 2

♥ A 8 6 3

Look at position 1 first. You have a combined holding of eight cards and the best chance of picking up the suit is to cash the king and then finesse dummy's jack. By doing so, you will succeed when the suit breaks 3-2 and West holds the queen. The alternative of cashing the king and ace ('playing for the drop', as it is called) is not nearly so good. It would gain when East holds queen doubleton but it would lose when West holds queen third, which is much more likely.

Position 2 is different. You have a combined holding of nine cards, making it much more likely that the queen is doubleton. The recommendation (from 'eight ever, nine never') is to spurn the finesse and play for the drop. This is indeed better but only marginally so.

Let's look at some situations where you should brush the 'eight ever, nine never' guideline firmly to one side.

Finessing to keep the danger hand off lead

We have seen in earlier chapters that one defender may be dangerous (he can cash tricks or lead through an honor), while the other may be safe. In such a situation you may not want to follow the 'nine never' rule. You will fare better by finessing into the safe hand. This deal is typical:

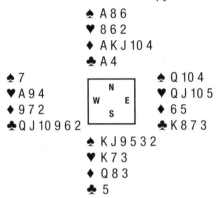

```
              ♠ A 8 6
              ♥ 8 6 2
              ♦ A K J 10 4
              ♣ A 4
   ♠ 7                        ♠ Q 10 4
   ♥ A 9 4         N          ♥ Q J 10 5
   ♦ 9 7 2      W     E       ♦ 6 5
   ♣ Q J 10 9 6 2   S         ♣ K 8 7 3
              ♠ K J 9 5 3 2
              ♥ K 7 3
              ♦ Q 8 3
              ♣ 5
```

West leads the ♣Q against your game in spades and you win with dummy's ace. What will happen if you mutter 'nine never' to yourself and play the ace and king of trumps? You will go down! When you turn to the diamond suit, East will ruff the third round and switch to the ♥Q. You will lose three hearts and a trump.

East is the danger hand here, because he can lead through your ♥K. To prevent him from gaining the lead you should finesse in trumps, even though you have nine cards in the suit. You cash the spade ace and finesse the jack. On this occasion the finesse wins and you will make no fewer than twelve tricks. Even if you had lost to a doubleton queen with West, you would have been sure of eleven tricks. West could not attack hearts successfully from his side and you would score five trumps, five diamonds and the club ace.

Playing for the drop to keep
the danger hand off lead

Similarly, it can be right to play for the drop, even when you hold only eight cards in the suit. As you probably guessed, this is the right play when a finesse would be into the danger hand. This deal is typical:

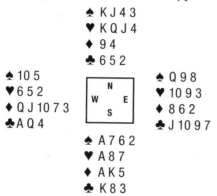

```
                    ♠ K J 4 3
                    ♥ K Q J 4
                    ♦ 9 4
                    ♣ 6 5 2
      ♠ 10 5                      ♠ Q 9 8
      ♥ 6 5 2         N           ♥ 10 9 3
      ♦ Q J 10 7 3  W   E         ♦ 8 6 2
      ♣ A Q 4         S           ♣ J 10 9 7
                    ♠ A 7 6 2
                    ♥ A 8 7
                    ♦ A K 5
                    ♣ K 8 3
```

West leads the ♦Q against your spade game. How will you play the trumps?

East is the danger hand, because he can lead through your ♣K. You win the diamond lead and cash the ace of trumps. What now? Perhaps you will whisper 'eight ever' and finesse the jack of trumps? It's not a good idea. When the cards lie as in the diagram, East will win and made a deadly switch to the ♣J. One down.

Instead you should rise with the king of trumps on the second round. This can gain in two ways. First of all, you may drop a doubleton queen from the East hand. Secondly, when East started with ♠Q-x-x and the queen does not drop, you can try your luck with three rounds of hearts. Here East will have to follow three times and you will get a club loser away on the fourth round, whether or not he chooses to ruff.

What if West started with Q-x-x in the trump suit and the finesse would have worked? You will still make the contract by playing for the drop! When the ♠Q does not fall, you turn to the heart suit as before. Even if West is able to ruff an early round of hearts, he cannot attack clubs successfully from his side. You are assured of ten tricks.

Finessing because a defender
is long in a side suit

When you hold nine cards it is a very close decision whether to play for the drop or to finesse. In the absence of any other information the relative odds are 52:48 in favor of playing for the drop. Once a player has shown length in a side suit, either in the auction or the early play, the odds may switch in favor of the finesse.

Here East has suggested a long suit by opening with a preemptive bid:

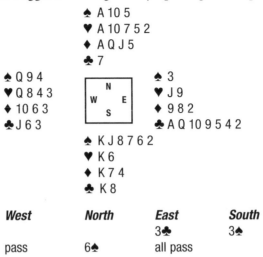

```
                    ♠ A 10 5
                    ♥ A 10 7 5 2
                    ♦ A Q J 5
                    ♣ 7
    ♠ Q 9 4              N            ♠ 3
    ♥ Q 8 4 3        W       E        ♥ J 9
    ♦ 10 6 3             S            ♦ 9 8 2
    ♣ J 6 3                           ♣ A Q 10 9 5 4 2
                    ♠ K J 8 7 6 2
                    ♥ K 6
                    ♦ K 7 4
                    ♣ K 8
```

West	North	East	South
		3♣	3♠
pass	6♠	all pass	

East wins the club lead and returns the ♦9. You must now pick up the trump suit. What play is best, do you think?

East is likely to hold seven clubs to his partner's three. In the other three suits West is likely to hold more cards than East. That's because he has more 'vacant spaces'. He started with ten non-clubs to East's six. This is more than enough to overturn the original 52:48 odds in favor of playing for the drop. You should cash the king of trumps and finesse dummy's ten.

There is another reason why you might choose to finesse against a queen with a combined holding of nine cards. That's when you can afford to lose a trump trick and a losing finesse (when trumps break 2-2) will still leave you with a trump in dummy to take a vital ruff later. Many players (muttering 'eight ever, nine never' under their breath) would go wrong on this deal:

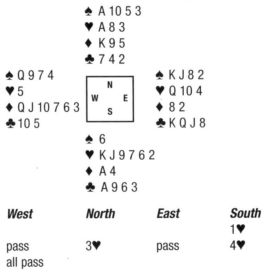

```
                    ♠ A 10 5 3
                    ♥ A 8 3
                    ♦ K 9 5
                    ♣ 7 4 2
    ♠ Q 9 7 4            N            ♠ K J 8 2
    ♥ 5              W       E        ♥ Q 10 4
    ♦ Q J 10 7 6 3      S            ♦ 8 2
    ♣ 10 5                            ♣ K Q J 8
                    ♠ 6
                    ♥ K J 9 7 6 2
                    ♦ A 4
                    ♣ A 9 6 3
```

West	North	East	South
			1♥
pass	3♥	pass	4♥
all pass			

West leads the ♦Q against your heart game and you win with the ace. Suppose you play the ace and king of trumps next. It's the best play in the trump suit, when looking at the suit in isolation. It does not give you the best chance of making this particular contract, though. The queen of trumps does not fall in two rounds and when East gains the lead in clubs he will draw dummy's last trump. The clubs are not 3-3 either and you end up with one trump loser and three club losers. One down!

A better play is to win with the ace of diamonds, cross to the ace of trumps and finesse the jack of trumps. If the finesse loses, trumps will have broken 2-2. The defenders will have no opportunity to remove dummy's last trump and you will be able to ruff the fourth round of clubs, if need be. When the cards lie as in the diagram, the trump finesse will win. Six trump tricks and four top winners in the side suits will bring the total to ten.

Here is another way to play this contract. Instead of drawing trumps, running the risk that one or other defender will be able to draw a third round of trumps before you take a club ruff, you play on clubs immediately. After ace and another club, you win the return and play a third club. You plan to play the ace and king of trumps before leading the fourth club. This line would succeed even if West started with queen third in the trump suit.

BY THE WAY

Look back at the full diagram and imagine that you had no problems whatsoever in the side suits and just needed to play the trump suit without losing two tricks there. Do you see the safety play? Playing the ace first is not safe because if West started with Q-10-x-x he would then score two trump tricks. Instead you should play the king first. If East shows out, you lead towards the dummy, forcing West to split his Q-10. If instead West shows out, you cross to the ace and lead back towards the jack.

Summary

✓ When you hold eight cards in a suit and are missing the queen, easily the best play is to finesse against the queen. When you hold nine cards it is better to play for the drop but the odds are close.

✓ On some hands it is better to play for the drop with eight cards. If the queen does not fall you keep the lead and can play for a discard.

✓ Similarly, it may be better to finesse with nine cards. That is when you are finessing into the safe hand and can therefore guarantee the contract.

EIGHT EVER, NINE NEVER

NOW TRY THESE...

1)

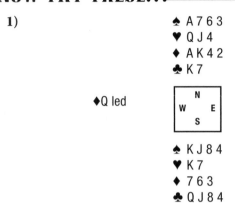

♠ A 7 6 3
♥ Q J 4
♦ A K 4 2
♣ K 7

♦Q led

♠ K J 8 4
♥ K 7
♦ 7 6 3
♣ Q J 8 4

West leads the ♦Q against your spade game. How will you play the contract?

2)

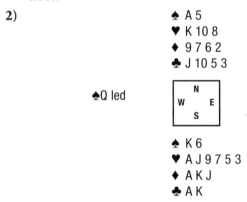

♠ A 5
♥ K 10 8
♦ 9 7 6 2
♣ J 10 5 3

♠Q led

♠ K 6
♥ A J 9 7 5 3
♦ A K J
♣ A K

You bid to a small slam in hearts and West leads the ♠Q. How will you play the contract?

3)

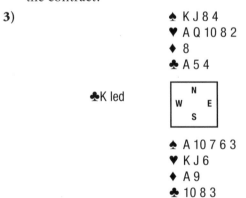

♠ K J 8 4
♥ A Q 10 8 2
♦ 8
♣ A 5 4

♣K led

♠ A 10 7 6 3
♥ K J 6
♦ A 9
♣ 10 8 3

You play in 6♠ after West has overcalled with an Unusual 2NT (showing 5-5 in the minors). How will you play the slam?

ANSWERS

1) Suppose you win the diamond lead, cash the ace of trumps and make the normal play in the trump suit by finessing the jack. If this loses, West will set up a diamond trick for the defenders and you will almost certainly go one down. A better idea is to play the ace and king of trumps. This will succeed immediately if West holds Q-x in the trump suit. If both defenders follow but the queen does not fall, you take advantage of the fact that you are still on lead by knocking out the ♥A. This will set up a discard for your potential diamond loser. (It is not safe to play a heart at Trick 2 because West may win and lead another diamond, perhaps allowing East to ruff dummy's remaining honor.)

2) With nine trumps it is normally right (by a small margin) to play for the drop. Here there is special reason for finessing East for the missing queen. You can arrange an end-play on West, should the finesse lose.

   Win the spade lead in your hand, play the two top clubs, cross to the king of trumps and play dummy's remaining top spade. When you lead a second round of trumps, let's assume first that East follows with a low card. Do you see why it is right to finesse now? If the finesse loses, West will have to give you a trick! A spade return will give you a ruff-and-discard. A diamond will be into your A-K-J and a club will be through dummy's J-10, guaranteeing you an extra trick whoever holds the ♣Q.

   Suppose next that East shows out on the second trump. Run dummy's card to West. If he finds the only safe return, a third trump, you will have to win in dummy and take the diamond finesse yourself.

3) With nine trumps you would normally play for the drop. Here, though, West's 2NT bid suggests that he has ten minor-suit cards to East's seven. That is enough to bring the odds in favor of finessing East for the ♠Q. Suppose West's shape were 2-1-5-5. He might then have led his singleton heart, seeking a ruff. The lack of a heart lead is further evidence that West's shape may be 1-2-5-5 instead.

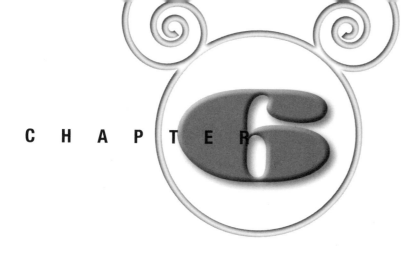

RUFF LOSERS IN THE DUMMY

 You will obviously gain by trumping losing cards in the weak hand. *J.B. Elwell*

It is generally a good idea to **ruff losers in the dummy**. Why is that? Because each ruff will give you an extra trick. Suppose this is your trump suit:

♠ A 6 5

♠ K Q J 10 3

You are certain to make five trump tricks but if you can take one ruff in dummy, you will bump this to six. Take two ruffs and you will make a total of seven trump tricks. There's not much direct benefit from taking ruffs in the South hand, of course. You would still make the five trump tricks that were yours initially.

Let's move straight away to some situations where you have the chance to ruff losers in the dummy but it is not a good idea to do so.

Ruffing a loser would kill an important entry

Sometimes you need to use dummy's trumps to reach the long cards in a side suit that you have established. Your plan is to establish the long suit and then draw trumps, ending in the dummy. This may not be possible if you have reduced the dummy's trump length by taking a ruff. Look at this deal:

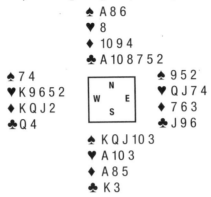

♠ A 8 6
♥ 8
♦ 10 9 4
♣ A 10 8 7 5 2

♠ 7 4
♥ K 9 6 5 2
♦ K Q J 2
♣ Q 4

♠ 9 5 2
♥ Q J 7 4
♦ 7 6 3
♣ J 9 6

♠ K Q J 10 3
♥ A 10 3
♦ A 8 5
♣ K 3

Impressed by your king in partner's club suit, you stretch to a small slam in spades. How should you play this contract when West leads the ♦K?

You can ruff two hearts in dummy but it won't do you much good. You will still be left with two diamond losers. A better plan is to set up dummy's club suit. Provided the suit breaks 3-2 you will set up discards for three of your four red-suit losers.

Let's see how the play goes. You win the diamond lead with the ace and play the king and queen of trumps, pleased to see the suit breaking 3-2. You then play the king and ace of clubs. It's your birthday! This suit breaks 3-2 as well. You ruff a third round of clubs with a high trump and return to dummy with the ♠A, claiming the contract.

Do you see why you would go down if you took even one heart ruff? You would not be able to draw trumps, ending in the dummy.

Ruffing a loser might prevent you from drawing trumps

Taking a ruff in dummy can sometimes spoil your communications in the trump suit, preventing you from drawing trumps thereafter. The original declarer played carelessly on this deal:

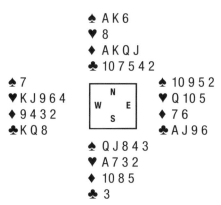

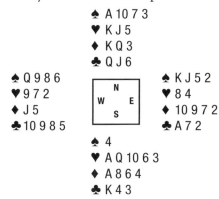

     West led the ♣K against the spade game. He continued with the ♣Q at Trick 2 and declarer ruffed. Not being one of those players who think it necessary to make a plan, South cashed the ♥A and ruffed a heart with the six of trumps. When he continued with the ace and king of trumps the 4-1 trump break came to light. It was no longer possible to make the contract. If declarer ruffed another club he would be left with fewer trumps than East. He tried his luck in diamonds instead, but East ruffed the third round. This left declarer with one trump loser, two hearts and a club.

     How should the hand have been played? Ten easy tricks are visible — five trumps, four diamonds and the ♥A. After ruffing the second round of clubs, declarer should play the ace and king of trumps. If the suit breaks 3-2 it will be safe to take a heart ruff for an overtrick. After scoring the ruff, declarer can return to his hand with a high club ruff to draw the last trump. If trumps break 4-1, as in the diagram, he will have to draw trumps and settle for ten tricks.

Ruffing losers in your hand works better

We saw earlier that taking a ruff in the long trump hand does not give you an extra trick. That's true in general but not when you can take so many ruffs that dummy ends with the longer trump holding. Such a style of play is known as 'reversing the dummy'. Here is an example:

You bid to a small slam in hearts and West leads the ♣10, covered by the queen and ace. Back comes a second round of clubs. If you decided to play on standard lines, you would draw two rounds of trumps and then play three top diamonds. You would need diamonds to break 3-3 or the defender with four diamonds also to hold the last trump (you could then cash three diamonds and ruff the fourth). This line of play would work when the sun was shining but not when the cards lie as in the diagram.

A better idea is to ruff three spades in the South hand. Win the club return with the king and play the king and ace of trumps, confirming that trumps break 3-2 (which you need for the dummy reversal to succeed). Cross to the ♠A and ruff a spade. Re-enter dummy twice in diamonds and ruff two more spades with high trumps. Return to dummy with the ♣J and draw West's last trump. You will make six winners in the side suits, three trump tricks in dummy and three ruffs in the South hand.

If trumps broke 4-1, you would have to abandon the dummy reversal and play on the original line mentioned above.

Summary

✓ A ruff in the short-trump hand gives you an extra trick; a ruff in the long-trump hand does not.

✓ Do not take a ruff in dummy when you need dummy's last trump as an entry to a suit that you plan to establish.

✓ Sometimes the best plan is to take several ruffs in the long-trump hand, eventually drawing trumps from the dummy. This is called a 'dummy reversal'.

RUFF LOSERS IN THE DUMMY

1)

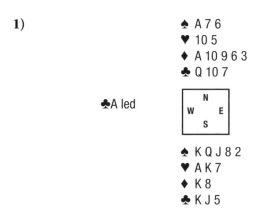

♠ A 7 6
♥ 10 5
♦ A 10 9 6 3
♣ Q 10 7

♣A led

♠ K Q J 8 2
♥ A K 7
♦ K 8
♣ K J 5

West leads the ♣A against your small slam in spades. How will you play the contract when he continues with a second club?

2)

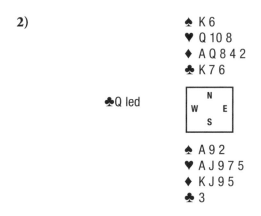

♠ K 6
♥ Q 10 8
♦ A Q 8 4 2
♣ K 7 6

♣Q led

♠ A 9 2
♥ A J 9 7 5
♦ K J 9 5
♣ 3

You bid to a small slam in hearts and West leads the ♣Q. You ruff the second club and see that you will need to find East with the ♥K. Will you take a spade ruff before drawing trumps? If not, why not?

ANSWERS

1) Your best chance of success is to ruff a heart in dummy. Should you ruff with a high trump or a low trump? (If you have not considered this point yet, look back at the problem and rethink your answer.) If you ruff with the ace of trumps, aiming to avoid an overruff from East, you will go down when the trumps divide 4-1. Such a break in the trump suit is much more likely than East being able to overruff in hearts, so you should ruff the third heart with a low trump. You can then draw trumps, in four rounds if necessary, and claim the contract.

2) There is no need to ruff a spade because your spade loser can eventually be thrown on the fifth round of diamonds. You may be wondering: what harm can a spade ruff do? It would prevent you from picking up a trump holding of king fourth in the East hand! With dummy reduced to just queen doubleton, you would be able to lead trumps from the dummy only twice. East would not cover with the king, of course, and would be left with an impregnable king doubleton. No more finesses would be possible.

FINESSE WHENEVER YOU CAN

 The subject of Finessing requires a knowledge of the particular situation, and there are many occasions when it is unwise to finesse. *J.B. Elwell*

A light comes to every beginner's eye the first time the finesse is explained. Wow, you can make an extra trick as easy as that! For the next few weeks, every time the dummy is laid out, the first thing they look for is an A-Q combination. Their guideline becomes: **finesse whenever you can**.

More experienced players regard the finesse differently. Firstly, you are not really gaining a trick. An A-Q poised over a king is just as good as an A-K and is worth two tricks anyway. Secondly, finesses do not always win. If your contract depends on a finesse, you may go down. Good players do not like relying on a finesse and will go to great lengths to avoid depending on mere fortune. Let's see some of the many situations where a finesse should not be taken.

The opening lead suggests the finesse will fail

Time after time you see players at Trick 1 taking finesses that cannot possibly succeed. By refusing the finesse they would often leave themselves with an alternative play. Take this common situation, for example:

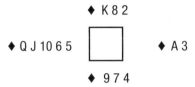

South reaches a major-suit game, let's say, and West leads the ♦Q. 'Play the king,' says declarer.

There is not one chance in a thousand that West holds the ♦A. Whoever heard of making such a lead against a suit contract? It is completely pointless for declarer to play dummy's king. Worse than that, it will actually cost a trick when East's ace is singleton or doubleton. The correct play is to duck, both on the first round and the second round. When the cards lie as in the diagram, the ace will appear and you will make a trick with the king. If the ace does not appear, there was nothing you could do about it anyway.

A similar situation arises on this deal:

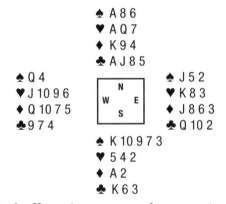

West leads the ♥J against your spade game. Are you tempted to finesse the queen? You shouldn't be, since it is unusual for defenders to lead from a K-J-10 combination against a suit contract.

Let's see what will happen if you do finesse dummy's ♥Q. East will win with the king and return the suit, establishing a second heart trick for the defenders. After drawing two rounds of trumps, you will have to take the club finesse. When this fails you will go down, losing one trump, two hearts and a club.

A much better idea is to rise with the ace of hearts at Trick 1. Even if West does hold the ♥K, this won't cost you very much. You can lead towards the ♥Q later, if necessary. You draw two rounds of trumps next, play the ♣K and finesse the ♣J. The finesse loses but East (the safe hand) is on lead and cannot play hearts successfully. Since the clubs break 3-3 you will be able to discard one of your heart losers.

It is too dangerous to finesse

Even when you have no clear indication that a finesse will fail, it may be too dangerous to take it. Take the South cards here:

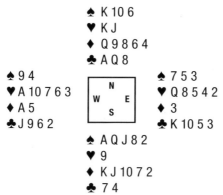

♠ K 10 6
♥ K J
♦ Q 9 8 6 4
♣ A Q 8

♠ 9 4
♥ A 10 7 6 3
♦ A 5
♣ J 9 6 2

♠ 7 5 3
♥ Q 8 5 4 2
♦ 3
♣ K 10 5 3

♠ A Q J 8 2
♥ 9
♦ K J 10 7 2
♣ 7 4

West leads the ♣2 against your game in spades. Since players are generally more willing to lead from a king than a jack, there is a fair chance that a club finesse will win. You should not take it, however, because by doing so you would risk the contract. As the cards lie, East would win with the king and switch to his singleton diamond, receiving a diamond ruff. The ♥A would then give the defenders four tricks.

If you rise with the ace of clubs at Trick 1, refusing the finesse, you are certain to make the contract (unless trumps break 5-0). You will simply draw trumps and knock out the ♦A — scoring five trump tricks, four diamonds and the ♣A.

In a suit contract you should be particularly wary of finessing when the opening lead is a spot card in a suit that has been bid by the dummy. The odds are high that the lead is a singleton. Look at this deal:

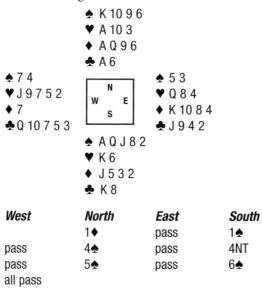

♠ K 10 9 6
♥ A 10 3
♦ A Q 9 6
♣ A 6

♠ 7 4
♥ J 9 7 5 2
♦ 7
♣ Q 10 7 5 3

♠ 5 3
♥ Q 8 4
♦ K 10 8 4
♣ J 9 4 2

♠ A Q J 8 2
♥ K 6
♦ J 5 3 2
♣ K 8

West	North	East	South
	1♦	pass	1♠
pass	4♠	pass	4NT
pass	5♠	pass	6♠
all pass			

West leads the ♦7 against your small slam in spades. How would you play the contract?

On bidding like this it would be normal for West to lead a heart or a club, hoping to cash or set up a trick before declarer could establish some discards. Why has West chosen to lead dummy's first-bid suit instead? It is very likely indeed that his ♦7 is a singleton. If you play low from dummy at Trick 1, East will win with the king and give his partner a diamond ruff. Not the best of starts!

Suppose instead that you rise with dummy's ace of diamonds at Trick 1. Can you see how to make the contract when East does hold K-10-8-4 in the diamond suit? It's not particularly easy but you must aim for what is known as an elimination play. You draw trumps and play the two winners in clubs, eliminating that suit. You then play the king and ace of hearts, ruffing the third round of hearts to eliminate that suit too. These cards will be left:

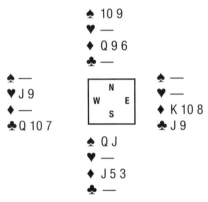

```
              ♠ 10 9
              ♥ —
              ♦ Q 9 6
              ♣ —
♠ —                        ♠ —
♥ J 9          N           ♥ —
♦ —        W     E         ♦ K 10 8
♣ Q 10 7       S           ♣ J 9
              ♠ Q J
              ♥ —
              ♦ J 5 3
              ♣ —
```

BY THE WAY

If West does not lead a diamond, you can guard against K-10-x-x with either defender. Draw trumps, eliminate hearts and clubs, and play a diamond to the queen. If east wins from K-10-x-x, he is endplayed. If the ♦Q wins, continue with a diamond towards the jack. If West started K-10-x-x, dummy's A-9 will now sit over his 10-x.

You now need to play the diamond suit in such a way that East cannot score more than one trick. Do you see how to do it?

You lead a low diamond to the queen, West showing out. If East wins with the king, he will have two losing options. He can lead away from the ♦10, allowing you to score the nine and jack separately. Alternatively, he can play a club, which will give you a ruff-and-discard. Either way, you will make the slam.

You can avoid a finesse with an endplay

One common way to avoid a finesse is to force the opponents to play the key suit for you. This is often possible in a suit contract, when you have plenty of trumps in both hands. You use the same style of play, known as 'elimination play', that we saw in the previous section. On the next deal many players would risk their slam by taking a heart finesse. An expert player (or even some aspiring but inexperienced player who happened to have read this book!) would follow a different line of play. See what you make of it:

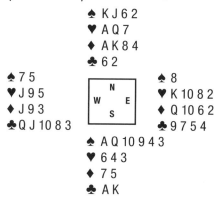

```
                    ♠ K J 6 2
                    ♥ A Q 7
                    ♦ A K 8 4
                    ♣ 6 2
     ♠ 7 5                          ♠ 8
     ♥ J 9 5        N               ♥ K 10 8 2
     ♦ J 9 3      W   E             ♦ Q 10 6 2
     ♣ Q J 10 8 3   S               ♣ 9 7 5 4
                    ♠ A Q 10 9 4 3
                    ♥ 6 4 3
                    ♦ 7 5
                    ♣ A K
```

You reach a small slam in spades and West leads the ♣Q. How good are your prospects, would you say? Does it seem to you that everything will depend on the heart finesse?

There is an extra chance — one that will succeed whenever East holds more diamonds than West. After winning the club lead you should draw trumps, cash the other club, play two top diamonds and ruff a diamond. You then return to dummy with a trump and lead the last diamond. When East produces the diamond queen, you do not ruff. You throw a heart away instead! East will then have to lead into dummy's ♥A-Q or play a third round of clubs, giving you a ruff-and-discard. Either way, you will make the contract without having to risk the heart finesse.

Summary

✓ Do not take a finesse when the opening lead suggests that it will fail. Look for some other way of making the contract.

✓ Do not take a finesse when this involves an unnecessary risk of defeat, should the finesse lose.

✓ You can often avoid taking a finesse by endplaying one of the defenders.

FINESSE WHENEVER YOU CAN

1)

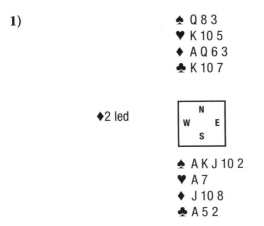

♠ Q 8 3
♥ K 10 5
♦ A Q 6 3
♣ K 10 7

♦2 led

♠ A K J 10 2
♥ A 7
♦ J 10 8
♣ A 5 2

West leads the ♦2 against your small slam in spades. Will you take the finesse? What is the reason for your decision?

2)

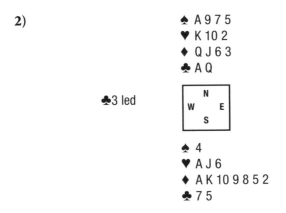

♠ A 9 7 5
♥ K 10 2
♦ Q J 6 3
♣ A Q

♣3 led

♠ 4
♥ A J 6
♦ A K 10 9 8 5 2
♣ 7 5

You bid to a small slam in diamonds and West leads the ♣3. Will you take the club finesse or not? What is the reason for your choice?

ANSWERS

1) What do you think West's diamond holding is? He may well have led from something like ♦K-9-5-2, in which case you can score an overtrick by finessing. There is another — more sinister — possibility. The lead may be a singleton! In that case a first-round finesse will lead to defeat. East will win with the king and give his partner a diamond ruff.

If you needed the diamond finesse to succeed, to give you any chance of making the slam, you would have to go ahead with it. That is not the case here. You should win with the ♦A and draw trumps. You can then knock out the ♦K, setting up a discard for your losing club.

Finessing risks going down. Rising with the ace guarantees the slam. Not a difficult choice!

2) Suppose you take the club finesse and it loses. You would then have to guess which defender held the ♥Q in order to make the slam. Good bridge players hate having to guess and on this deal there is no need to. You should win with the ♣A and set about eliminating the spade suit. (Eliminate means 'remove', generally in preparation for an endplay.) You cross to the ace of spades and ruff a spade. A trump to dummy is followed by a second spade ruff. You draw the outstanding trump(s), ending in dummy and ruff dummy's last spade. An end position similar to this will be left:

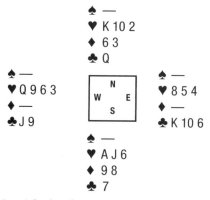

You now exit with the ♣Q. You are certain to make the slam, whoever wins with the ♣K. That defender will have to play a heart for you, sparing you a guess in the suit, or give you a ruff-and-discard. Twelve tricks either way!

C H A P T E R 8

PLAY ON YOUR LONGEST SUIT FIRST

 To bring in two suits is, of course, a delightful sensation, but it is a great deal better to confine your efforts to bring in one sure suit than to attempt two with the result of getting neither. *J.B. Elwell*

You are about to play in 3NT and you see that you do not have nine top tricks available. Which suit will you play on? Very often, you will follow the guideline: **play on your longest suit first**. It will work well here:

```
                    ♠ 9 4 3
                    ♥ A 7
                    ♦ K J 7 4 2
                    ♣ Q J 4
   ♠ Q 10 8 6 2        ┌─────┐        ♠ J 7 5
   ♥ 9 8 6 4          N│     │        ♥ J 10 5 2
   ♦ A 5           W   │     │   E    ♦ 9 6
   ♣ 5 3              S│     │        ♣ A 9 7 6
                       └─────┘
                    ♠ A K
                    ♥ K Q 3
                    ♦ Q 10 8 3
                    ♣ K 10 8 2
```

Partner raises your 1NT opening to 3NT and West leads the ♠6 to his partner's jack. You win in the South hand and see that you have only five top tricks. Since you need four more tricks to bump this to nine, it makes good sense to play on the longest suit available to you — diamonds. By knocking out the ace of diamonds you will make the contract. If instead you played on clubs, the defenders would win with the ace and clear the spades, leaving you one trick short.

However, there are many occasions when it is not right to play on the longest suit first. Let's see the most important of them.

Playing on the longest suit will be too slow

Sometimes it is not practical to play on your longest suit because you have two stoppers to knock out there and the defenders will cash five tricks, beating your 3NT, before you can take your nine. That is what 'too slow' means. The line of play will generate the required number of tricks all right, but the defenders will make too many tricks first.

This deal illustrates the situation:

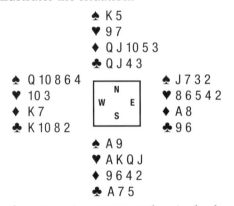

```
              ♠ K 5
              ♥ 9 7
              ♦ Q J 10 5 3
              ♣ Q J 4 3
♠ Q 10 8 6 4    ┌─────┐      ♠ J 7 3 2
♥ 10 3          │   N │      ♥ 8 6 5 4 2
♦ K 7         W │     │ E    ♦ A 8
♣ K 10 8 2      │ S   │      ♣ 9 6
                └─────┘
              ♠ A 9
              ♥ A K Q J
              ♦ 9 6 4 2
              ♣ A 7 5
```

West leads the ♠6 against 3NT. What is the best chance of making nine tricks?

Suppose you win with the spade ace and attack your longest suit, playing a diamond. The defenders will win and play another spade, removing your last protection in the suit. Hopeless, isn't it? If you play another diamond you will set up enough tricks for the contract but the opponents will beat you to the tape, cashing three spades and two diamonds.

How should you play the contract? You start with seven top tricks. No more are available from the majors and we have just seen what will happen if you play on diamonds. The extra two tricks you need will have to come from the club suit. You will need West to hold the king of clubs or clubs to divide 3-3. Cash the ace of clubs and play a low club to dummy's queen. If the queen wins the trick, return to your hand with the ace of hearts and lead another club towards dummy. When the cards lie as in our diagram, West will doubtless rise with the king on the third round and play another spade. Since you won the first spade trick in your hand, with the ace, dummy's king of spades will provide an entry to the established jack of clubs. Nine tricks are yours.

Playing on the longest suit first risks defeat

By the time you have to decide which suit to play on, one of the defenders may be 'safe' (you can afford it if he gains the lead), the other may be 'dangerous' (he will beat the contract if he gains the lead). As a result, it may be risky to play on your longest suit and perfectly safe to play on a different suit. Take the South seat on this deal:

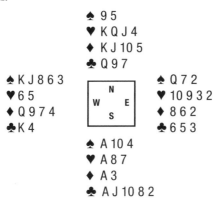

```
                ♠ 9 5
                ♥ K Q J 4
                ♦ K J 10 5
                ♣ Q 9 7
 ♠ K J 8 6 3          N          ♠ Q 7 2
 ♥ 6 5          W         E      ♥ 10 9 3 2
 ♦ Q 9 7 4           S          ♦ 8 6 2
 ♣ K 4                          ♣ 6 5 3
                ♠ A 10 4
                ♥ A 8 7
                ♦ A 3
                ♣ A J 10 8 2
```

You play in 3NT and West leads the ♠6 to his partner's queen. When you hold up the ♠A the defenders persist with spades and you win the third round. What now?

As always your first move in a notrump contract is to count the top tricks. Here the total comes to eight, only one short. How should you seek your ninth trick? Crossing to dummy and taking a club finesse is not attractive. The finesse is into the 'danger hand'. If it loses, West will cash two more spades and you will go down.

What alternative is there to playing on clubs, your longest suit? You could play the ♦A and finesse dummy's ♦J. If that loses, the safe hand will gain the lead. He will not be able to beat the contract and you will have nine tricks to take when you regain the lead.

BY THE WAY

Even if dummy's diamonds were only K-J-5 it would be correct to finesse in that suit first. East could not damage you if the finesse failed and you would be able to take the club finesse when you regained the lead. You would make the contract if either finesse was right!

When the suit that has been led is divided 5-3, it is not always the defender with the five-card length who is dangerous. When you have a partial stopper left after Trick 1, you may want to prevent the other defender from leading through it. That is the case here:

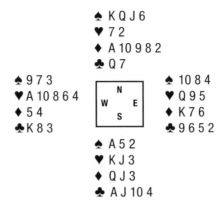

♠ K Q J 6
♥ 7 2
♦ A 10 9 8 2
♣ Q 7

♠ 9 7 3
♥ A 10 8 6 4
♦ 5 4
♣ K 8 3

♠ 10 8 4
♥ Q 9 5
♦ K 7 6
♣ 9 6 5 2

♠ A 5 2
♥ K J 3
♦ Q J 3
♣ A J 10 4

West leads the ♥6 against your 3NT contract and East plays the queen. What line of play will give you the best chance of making the contract?

The first point to note is that a hold-up (allowing East's queen to win) will not work at all against competent defenders. East will continue with a second heart and West will allow your honor to win the second round of the suit. With the defenders' communications intact, you will not be able to lose the lead to either hand!

So, you win the first trick with the king. What next? Your J-3 will act as a second stopper in the heart suit, provided it is West who gains the lead rather than East. In other words, it is East who is the danger hand. Suppose you take a diamond finesse, playing on your longest suit, and the finesse loses. East will return his last heart, through your jack, and you will go down. Instead you should cross to dummy with the king of spades. You then lead the queen of clubs, running this card into the safe West hand. The finesse loses, as it happens, but you don't mind in the least. West cannot continue hearts profitably and on any other return you will claim four spades, one heart, one diamond and three clubs. If West plays a diamond, of course, you will rise with dummy's ace. With nine top tricks already established, it would be foolish to put the contract at risk by playing low.

Playing on the longest suit first does not attack an entry

On the deal that we have just seen, you had to remove only one enemy stopper to make the contract. Much of the time you will have two stoppers to dislodge and must decide which one to attack first. The general rule is: **attack first the entry to the danger hand**. By the time you play on your second suit, it will be the safe hand who will gain the lead. He can do you no damage.

Too hard to visualize without an example deal? You could be right! Try this for size:

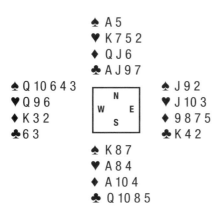

♠ A 5
♥ K 7 5 2
♦ Q J 6
♣ A J 9 7

♠ Q 10 6 4 3   ♠ J 9 2
♥ Q 9 6   ♥ J 10 3
♦ K 3 2   ♦ 9 8 7 5
♣ 6 3   ♣ K 4 2

♠ K 8 7
♥ A 8 4
♦ A 10 4
♣ Q 10 8 5

West leads the ♠4 against your 3NT. How should you plan the play?

You can count six top tricks and playing on clubs, your longest suit, would bump this to nine tricks if the finesse won. Think for a moment what would happen if the club finesse lost. East would clear the spades and even if you held up the ♠K until the third round, the contract would still be at risk. When you sought a ninth trick via a diamond finesse, this play would be into the danger hand. If that finesse lost too, West would cash two spade tricks to beat the contract.

Since the diamond finesse risks West gaining the lead and the club finesse does not, you should play on diamonds first. Win the spade lead with the ace and run the ♦Q. The finesse loses and West returns the queen of spades. You hold up the king and win the third round of spades. East has now become the 'safe hand'. The club finesse loses, as it happens, but East has no spade to play. (If he did, the suit would have broken 4-4 and would pose no threat.) Nine tricks are assured.

Suppose we alter the deal slightly, giving North the ♣K instead of the ♣A:

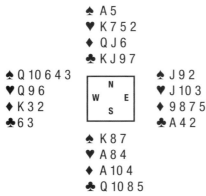

♠ A 5
♥ K 7 5 2
♦ Q J 6
♣ K J 9 7

♠ Q 10 6 4 3   ♠ J 9 2
♥ Q 9 6   ♥ J 10 3
♦ K 3 2   ♦ 9 8 7 5
♣ 6 3   ♣ A 4 2

♠ K 8 7
♥ A 8 4
♦ A 10 4
♣ Q 10 8 5

Again you play in 3NT, win West's spade lead and must calculate which minor suit to play first.

The contract is at risk only when West (the danger hand) holds the ♦K. You should therefore attack that suit first. The diamond finesse loses, as it happens, and West clears the spades. When you play on clubs, your luck turns. East, the safe hand, wins the trick and you make the contract.

Go through the play again, this time playing on clubs first. East wins with the ace and clears the spades. When the diamond finesse loses, West will cash two long spades to put you down.

It's a valuable and important guideline: when you may need to knock out two enemy stoppers, attack the potential entry to the danger hand first.

Summary

✓ In a notrump contract it is often right to play on your longest suit first. That's because it will usually yield the most extra tricks.

✓ When there are two different suits that each may yield sufficient extra tricks, turn to the suit that offers greater safety. Playing one suit may risk losing the lead to the danger hand; playing on the other may not.

✓ When you must play on two different suits to establish enough tricks for the contract, normally attack first the suit where the danger hand may have an entry. By the time you play on the second suit, the other defender may have become safe.

PLAY ON YOUR LONGEST SUIT FIRST

NOW TRY THESE...

1)

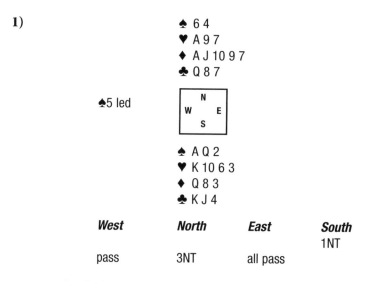

♠ 6 4
♥ A 9 7
♦ A J 10 9 7
♣ Q 8 7

♠5 led

| N |
| W E |
| S |

♠ A Q 2
♥ K 10 6 3
♦ Q 8 3
♣ K J 4

West	*North*	*East*	*South*
			1NT
pass	3NT	all pass	

West leads the ♠5 and East plays the jack, won with the queen. What will you do next?

2)

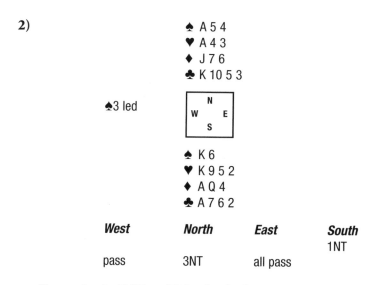

♠ A 5 4
♥ A 4 3
♦ J 7 6
♣ K 10 5 3

♠3 led

| N |
| W E |
| S |

♠ K 6
♥ K 9 5 2
♦ A Q 4
♣ A 7 6 2

West	*North*	*East*	*South*
			1NT
pass	3NT	all pass	

You arrive in 3NT and West leads the ♠3. How will you play the hand?

ANSWERS

1) Suppose you play on the long suit first, running the ♦Q. Your contract will be in danger if the finesse loses and East clears the spade suit. With only eight top tricks at your disposal, you will have to play on clubs and will go down when West (the danger hand) holds the ♣A. A better idea is to play on clubs first, attacking the potential entry to the danger hand. If the defenders win immediately and revert to spades, you will hold up the ace until the third round. You can then relax and finesse diamonds into the safe (East) hand.

What should you do if you play on clubs and the defenders allow the first round of clubs to win? With a club trick in the bag you can ensure the contract by taking the diamond finesse. Even if it loses, you will have nine tricks.

2) You have seven top tricks and should aim to score one more trick in each of the minors. In clubs, you have a good chance of setting up a long card without letting West on play. (You will cash the ace and then play low to the ten unless an honor appears from West.) In diamonds there is about a 50% chance that the finesse will lose and West will gain the lead.

You should 'attack the entry to the danger hand' by playing diamonds first. Win the spade lead with the king, cross to the ♥A and play a diamond to the queen. If the diamond finesse wins, turn to the club suit. If the diamond finesse loses, hold up the ♠A until the third round and play clubs in the suggested manner, hoping to keep West off lead.

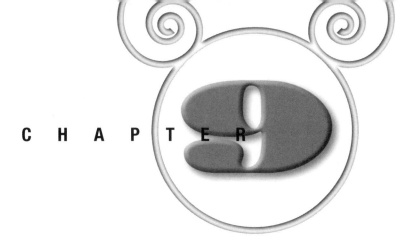

LEAD TOWARDS HIGH CARDS

As declarer, take a mental stock of the cards you hold early in the hand, and decide from which hand each combination should be led. *J.B. Elwell*

One of the basic fundamentals of cardplay is that **you should lead towards high cards**. These are basic positions, in every book for beginners:

1) ♠ K 5   2) ♥ A Q   3) ♦ K J 6
   ☐   ☐   ☐
   ♠ 8 3   ♥ 7 4   ♦ 8 5 2

Lead towards the king in Position 1 and you will make a trick whenever West holds the ace. Position 2 is the familiar ace-queen finesse where again you must lead towards the honor that you are hoping to make. In Position 3 you will lead low to the jack, hoping that it will win or force the ace. If the jack loses to the queen, you will later lead low to the king.

In all three positions your prospects of extra tricks will be negligible if you lead away from the high cards instead of towards them.

Even when you hold honors in both hands there may be benefit in leading towards the stronger holding. Look at this situation:

♠ K J 7 2

♠ A 8   ♠ 10 9 6 3

♠ Q 5 4

What is the best way to seek three spade tricks? The cat next door will manage it when the suit divides 3-3. What chance do you have against a 4-2 break? You should lead low to the jack; if that wins, return to your hand in another suit and lead low to the king. Whenever West started with a doubleton ace he will waste it on a low card. Each of your honors will then score a trick.

Perhaps you are wondering why you should play West for a doubleton ace rather than East. Suppose the cards lie like this instead:

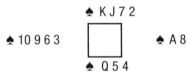

♠ K J 7 2

♠ 10 9 6 3   ♠ A 8

♠ Q 5 4

If you could see the defenders' cards you could lead low towards the queen and duck the next round. But this play is hardly practical since you would then lose two tricks when the suit broke 3-3!

The basic purpose of leading towards high cards is clear. You force the player in second seat to commit himself before you choose your play from the hand sitting over him. The time has come for us to look at some situations where this rule should be broken.

Leading from high cards in dummy may tempt a defender to rise

When you lead towards the dummy, the defender playing second to the trick can see what cards lie over him. When you lead towards the closed hand, it is much more difficult for the defender in second seat. He does not know what cards lie over him and you may be able to turn this to your advantage.

How would you play this slam?

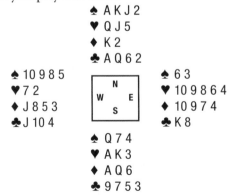

♠ A K J 2
♥ Q J 5
♦ K 2
♣ A Q 6 2

♠ 10 9 8 5   ♠ 6 3
♥ 7 2   ♥ 10 9 8 6 4
♦ J 8 5 3   ♦ 10 9 7 4
♣ J 10 4   ♣ K 8

♠ Q 7 4
♥ A K 3
♦ A Q 6
♣ 9 7 5 3

West leads the ♠10 against 6NT. You have ten tricks outside clubs and therefore need two club tricks. How would you play the slam?

'Are you joking?' many players would say. 'I take the club finesse!'

This will give you a 50% chance, yes, but you can do better. A small improvement is available by cashing the ♣A before crossing back to hand and leading towards the ♣Q. This would work wonders when East held a singleton king. An even better idea is to win the spade lead in dummy and immediately lead a low club away from the ace-queen. What do you think East will do with a doubleton king? An expert would be familiar with the situation and would play low smoothly, baring the king. Most of the world's defenders are not up to this — nowhere near! They will rise with the king, scared that you are about to play the jack and later drop their king. Meanwhile if your club play does not smoke out the king, you can take the finesse on the next round.

Leading away from high cards is the only chance

Sometimes you can tell that leading towards high cards is destined to fail:

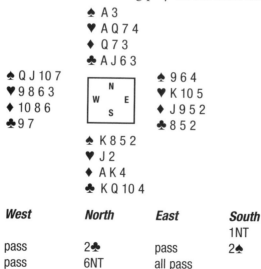

```
              ♦ K Q 5 2
  ♦ 8 7 4       ┌───┐       ♦ A J 9 6
              └───┘
              ♦ 10 3
```

Suppose you need two diamond tricks, and you can tell from the bidding that East holds the ♦A; it is pointless to lead towards the K-Q, playing West for the ace. If you can afford to lose the lead twice, lead towards the ♦10 instead. When East holds the jack you will make two diamond tricks, whether he plays it on the first round or not. The winning play on the next deal is similar:

```
                  ♠ A 3
                  ♥ A Q 7 4
                  ♦ Q 7 3
                  ♣ A J 6 3
  ♠ Q J 10 7                      ♠ 9 6 4
  ♥ 9 8 6 3       ┌─────┐         ♥ K 10 5
  ♦ 10 8 6        │  N  │         ♦ J 9 5 2
  ♣ 9 7           │W   E│         ♣ 8 5 2
                  │  S  │
                  └─────┘
                  ♠ K 8 5 2
                  ♥ J 2
                  ♦ A K 4
                  ♣ K Q 10 4
```

West	North	East	South
			1NT
pass	2♣	pass	2♠
pass	6NT	all pass	

How would you play 6NT when West leads the ♠Q?

There are nine top tricks in spades, diamonds and clubs. To bring your total to twelve, you will need three more from the heart suit. How will the suit have to lie for this to be possible? If West has the ♥K you cannot make three heart tricks (unless the king is singleton). You need East to have king third or king doubleton in hearts.

It's no use leading the ♥2 to the queen. East will win and you will have no chance whatsoever of a third heart trick. Instead you should lead low from dummy towards the jack. East has no answer to this play. If he rises with the king each of your three honors will score a trick. He will doubtless play low, allowing the jack to win. You will then duck the second round of hearts. The ace will subsequently drop the king and the ♥Q will give you the slam.

Summary

✓ As bridge myths go, 'always lead towards strength' is a good one! By leading towards honors, you force the defender in the second seat to commit himself before you have expended a high card.

✓ It is sometimes beneficial to lead away from a strong holding in dummy. The defender sitting over the dummy may lose his nerve and rise with an honor unnecessarily. Sometimes he will have no winning option.

LEAD TOWARDS HIGH CARDS

NOW TRY THESE...

1)

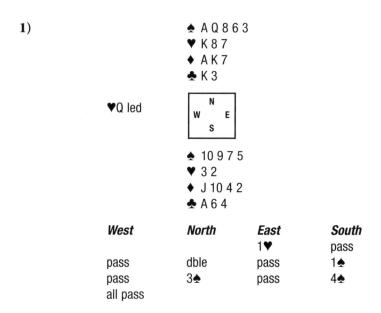

♠ A Q 8 6 3
♥ K 8 7
♦ A K 7
♣ K 3

♥Q led

♠ 10 9 7 5
♥ 3 2
♦ J 10 4 2
♣ A 6 4

West	North	East	South
		1♥	pass
pass	dble	pass	1♠
pass	3♠	pass	4♠
all pass			

The defenders play three rounds of hearts (East had the ace). You ruff the third round and find that West started with ♥Q-J-4. How will you play 4♠? In particular, how will you play the trump suit? Can you tell which defender holds the ♠K?

2)

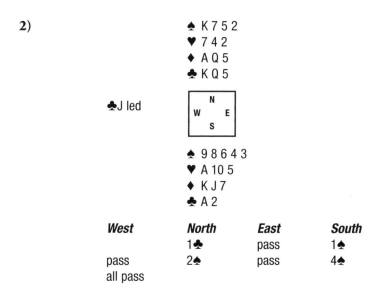

♠ K 7 5 2
♥ 7 4 2
♦ A Q 5
♣ K Q 5

♣J led

♠ 9 8 6 4 3
♥ A 10 5
♦ K J 7
♣ A 2

West	North	East	South
	1♣	pass	1♠
pass	2♠	pass	4♠
all pass			

West leads the ♣J against your spade game. What is your plan?

ANSWERS

1) The normal way to play this spade holding is to 'lead towards strength', playing a low card from the South hand and finessing the queen. However, East opened the bidding and West has shown up with three points already. Since West failed to respond despite holding ♥Q-J-4, you can be certain that East holds the ♠K. You should therefore abandon any ideas of taking a trump finesse.

   After ruffing the third round of hearts, play a trump to the ace. If the ♠K falls singleton from East, return to your hand with a club to finesse against West's ♠J. Otherwise play East for a doubleton ♠K and attempt to endplay him. Play the two top clubs and ruff a club, eliminating that suit. You then exit with a trump. The full deal may look like this:

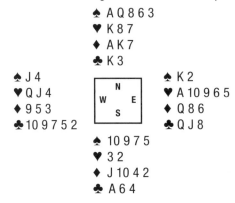

```
              ♠ A Q 8 6 3
              ♥ K 8 7
              ♦ A K 7
              ♣ K 3
  ♠ J 4                        ♠ K 2
  ♥ Q J 4          N           ♥ A 10 9 6 5
  ♦ 9 5 3      W     E         ♦ Q 8 6
  ♣ 10 9 7 5 2      S          ♣ Q J 8
              ♠ 10 9 7 5
              ♥ 3 2
              ♦ J 10 4 2
              ♣ A 6 4
```

   When East wins with the bare ♠K he will have to give you a ruff-and-discard or lead a diamond away from the queen. You make your game either way.

2) One of your heart losers can be thrown on dummy's third club, so your sole concern is to avoid three trump losers. If you play a trump to the king on the first round, you will go down when East holds singleton ace. The safety play is to duck the first round of spades in both hands and then lead towards the king on the second round. If the defenders switch to hearts when you duck a trump, you will play three rounds of clubs to discard a heart before playing on trumps again.

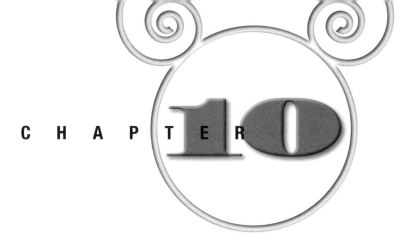

RUFF THE DEFENDERS' WINNERS

 The greatest weakness and the most expensive fault in the beginner's game is his predilection for trumping in the strong trump hand. *J.B. Elwell*

What would you say are the two main advantages of playing in a trump contract rather than in notrump? The first is that you can score extra tricks by ruffing in the short trump hand. The second, just as important, is that you can **ruff the defenders' winners**, preventing them from running their strongest suit.

This deal illustrates the dual power of the trump suit:

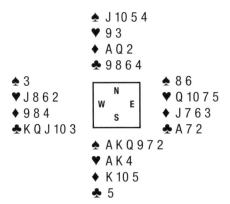

In a notrump contract the defenders would score the first five club tricks, preventing you from even scoring a game. If instead you play in spades, you can make a slam. You can ruff the second round of clubs, restricting the defenders to just one trick there. You can then score an extra trump trick by ruffing a heart in the short trump hand.

There are various situations where you have the chance to ruff a defender's winner but you should not do so. Let's have a look at them.

Ruffing would cause you to lose control

When you would have to ruff the defender's winner in your longer trump holding, there is often a worry about keeping trump control. Perhaps one of the defenders holds four trumps. If you take a ruff now you may be forced to ruff again later, leaving the defender with more trumps than you. This type of hand occurs frequently:

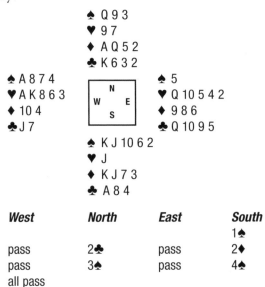

West	North	East	South
			1♠
pass	2♣	pass	2♦
pass	3♠	pass	4♠
all pass			

You arrive in 4♠ and West launches the defense with the ace and king of hearts. What should you do?

Suppose first that you ruff the second heart. You will then be down to the same number of trumps as West. When you play on trumps a strong defender in the West seat will refuse to win either of the first two rounds. (If he did, you would be able to ruff a third round of hearts in the dummy.)

West will then hold A-8 of trumps over your J-10 and there will be no way to make the contract. If you play a third round of trumps, West can win and force your last trump with a heart. If instead you play on diamonds, West will ruff and cash the ace of trumps. You will be left with a loser in the club suit for one down.

How can you avoid this unseemly end? By refusing to ruff in the long trump hand at Trick 2! Instead you should discard your club loser. If West perseveres with yet another heart you can ruff in the dummy, the short trump hand. Since you still have five trumps in your hand, against the four that West holds, you will be in no danger of losing control of the hand.

The next deal is on a similar theme — resisting a force by refusing to ruff. In this example the refusal to ruff has the effect of exhausting one defender of the suit led:

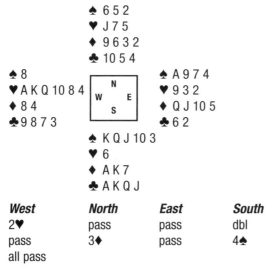

West	North	East	South
2♥	pass	pass	dbl
pass	3♦	pass	4♠
all pass			

West, who opened the bidding with a weak two in hearts, leads the king of hearts, followed by the ace. How will you play the spade game?

Let's see what happens first if you ruff the second heart. You continue with the king of trumps and East allows this to win. He ducks again when the queen of trumps is led. What now? The answer is that you will go down. If you lead a third round of trumps, East will win and force your last trump with a third round of hearts. You will then lose two trump tricks, as well as a diamond and a heart. (It's no good throwing a diamond loser on the third round of hearts because West will win and play yet another heart.)

The only way to make the contract is to discard your diamond loser on the second round of hearts. You cannot discard again when another heart is played, or you would lose three hearts and the trump ace. You ruff, therefore, bringing yourself down to four trumps — the same as East. Since East has no hearts left, you can play on trumps until he takes the trump ace. You then win his return and draw his last trump.

Ruffing in the short trump hand would kill an entry

Even when the ruff will be in the short trump hand, it can be dangerous to take it. One reason may be that you plan to establish a long suit in dummy and the only entry to the long cards lies in the trump suit. That's the case here:

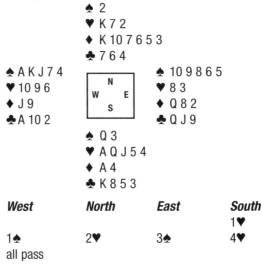

West	North	East	South
			1♥
1♠	2♥	3♠	4♥
all pass			

West allows you to play 4♥, and leads a top spade. A club switch at Trick 2 would make life very easy for you. If West switches to a red suit you will be able to ruff the diamonds good (ruffing high) and draw trumps, ending in the dummy. The only tricky continuation from West is a second top spade. How would you play the contract then?

If you ruff the second spade, reducing the dummy to two trumps, you will not be able to enjoy dummy's diamond suit. You could ruff the diamonds good but you would not be able to draw trumps, ending in the dummy. To counter West's defense you must discard a club on the second top spade. A further spade can do you no damage, since you can ruff in your hand; with diamonds and hearts both 3-2, the contract is now guaranteed.

Ruffing would permit an overruff

The final reason why you might refuse to ruff a defender's winner is that you expect to be overruffed:

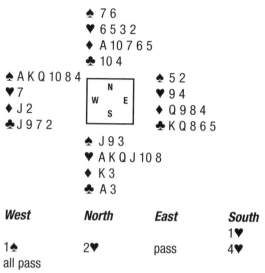

```
                    ♠ 7 6
                    ♥ 6 5 3 2
                    ♦ A 10 7 6 5
                    ♣ 10 4
♠ A K Q 10 8 4              ♠ 5 2
♥ 7                         ♥ 9 4
♦ J 2                       ♦ Q 9 8 4
♣ J 9 7 2                   ♣ K Q 8 6 5
                    ♠ J 9 3
                    ♥ A K Q J 10 8
                    ♦ K 3
                    ♣ A 3
```

West	North	East	South
			1♥
1♠	2♥	pass	4♥
all pass			

West cashes two top spades, East playing high-low, and continues with a third spade. If you ruff in the dummy, there is a fair chance that East will over-ruff. The eventual club loser will put you one down. Instead you should discard a club from dummy on the third round of spades. You will then be able to ruff a club in dummy instead of a spade! This technique is known as 'trading ruffs'. You swap a dangerous spade ruff for a safe club ruff.

Summary

✓ Playing in a trump contract gives you two big advantages: you can score extra tricks by ruffing in the dummy, and you can ruff to prevent the defenders from scoring tricks in own suits.

✓ You can sometimes maintain trump control by refusing to ruff in the long trump hand until the ruff can be taken in the short trump hand.

✓ When you plan to establish a side suit in dummy, using the trump suit for re-entry, be wary of ruffing in the short trump hand. You may no longer be able to draw trumps, ending in the dummy.

RUFF THE DEFENDERS' WINNERS

NOW TRY THESE...

1)

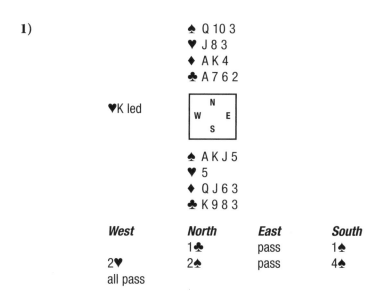

♠ Q 10 3
♥ J 8 3
♦ A K 4
♣ A 7 6 2

♥K led

♠ A K J 5
♥ 5
♦ Q J 6 3
♣ K 9 8 3

West	North	East	South
	1♣	pass	1♠
2♥	2♠	pass	4♠
all pass			

You reach game in spades, on a 4-3 fit, and West leads the ♥K followed by the ♥Q. How will you play the contract?

2)

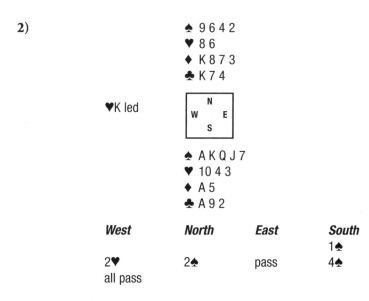

♠ 9 6 4 2
♥ 8 6
♦ K 8 7 3
♣ K 7 4

♥K led

♠ A K Q J 7
♥ 10 4 3
♦ A 5
♣ A 9 2

West	North	East	South
			1♠
2♥	2♠	pass	4♠
all pass			

West cashes the king and ace of hearts, East playing the seven followed by the five. At Trick 3 West continues with the queen of hearts. Will you ruff this trick or not? If you do decide to ruff, which of dummy's trumps will you use?

ANSWERS

1) Suppose you ruff the second heart and play three rounds of trumps. You are unlikely to make the contract unless the trumps break 3-3. A better idea is to throw a club on the second round of hearts. If the defenders persist with hearts, as is likely, you will throw another club. A fourth round of hearts will do the defenders no good because you will be able to ruff high in the dummy — in the short trump holding. Whatever the defenders do, after scoring three heart tricks, you will be able to draw four rounds of trumps and make your contract even when trumps break 4-2.

2) It is quite likely that hearts are 6-2 and that East is poised to overruff the dummy. This may be the layout:

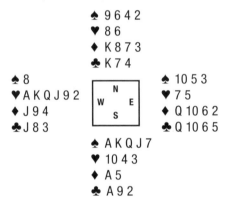

If you are determined to ruff the third heart in dummy, you should ruff with the nine. This would allow you to make the contract when West held the ♠10 and East could not overruff. However, there is a much better play available. On the third round of hearts you should discard a club from dummy! Whatever West plays next, you will win and draw trumps. You will then be able to ruff a club in dummy for your tenth trick.

C H A P T E R **11**

LEAD LOW TO A TRICK

 If you want high cards to fall, lead high cards. *J.B. Elwell*

It is generally beneficial to **lead a low card to a trick**. If the next player chooses to play an honor, or is forced to play an honor, he will capture nothing with it. Look at this common position:

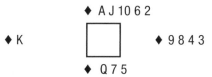

♦ A J 10 6 2

♦ K   ♦ 9 8 4 3

♦ Q 7 5

If you lead the queen on the first round, West's king will not die in vain. The first round of the suit will consume the queen, king and ace, promoting East's ♦9 to win the fourth round. Instead you should lead low from the South hand. You capture West's king with the ace and bring in the whole suit. The guideline worth remembering is 'do not lead a high card to a trick unless you can afford it to be covered'.

Here is another position where many players go wrong:

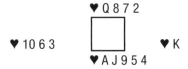

♥ Q 8 7 2

♥ 10 6 3   ♥ K

♥ A J 9 5 4

You plan to finesse East for the ♥K. All will be easy if the suit breaks 2-2. You can also pick up a singleton ten with West or a singleton king with East. Some players lead the queen from the North hand, expecting to be congratulated if this pins a singleton ten with West. Leading the queen is a poor play that would cost a trick when East holds a singleton king. Best is to play low to the jack, which caters for both cases. If the ten appears from West you can return to dummy in some other suit and play low to the nine on the next round.

It's time to see some situations where it is right to lead a high card to a trick.

Lead high to retain the lead

When entries to one hand or other are scarce, you may be forced to lead an honor where you would otherwise lead low.

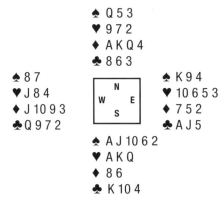

```
              ♠ Q 5 3
              ♥ 9 7 2
              ♦ A K Q 4
              ♣ 8 6 3
♠ 8 7                        ♠ K 9 4
♥ J 8 4          N           ♥ 10 6 5 3
♦ J 10 9 3    W     E        ♦ 7 5 2
♣ Q 9 7 2        S           ♣ A J 5
              ♠ A J 10 6 2
              ♥ A K Q
              ♦ 8 6
              ♣ K 10 4
```

You overbid to 6♠ and West leads the ♦J, won with the ace. Looking at the trump suit in isolation, you would prefer to lead a low trump from dummy. You would then avoid a trump loser if East held a singleton king. It's not a good idea here! If you lead low and win the first round of trumps with the jack, you could pick up East's remaining K-9 in trumps only by using dummy's remaining entry in diamonds for a second trump lead. Unable to lead towards the ♣K later in the hand, you would then go down.

Since you need the remaining diamond entry to play on clubs, you should lead the queen on the first round of trumps. If East chooses not to cover, you will still be in dummy to repeat the trump finesse. After drawing trumps, you can cross to the ♦K, cash the ♦Q to throw one club and then lead towards the ♣K. What a shame it would be to go down when both finesses were right!

Lead high to give yourself an extra chance

We saw a few moments ago that you should not lead high when you are missing four cards to the king and ten. Somewhat strangely, the situation is different when you are missing only three cards to the king and ten:

You can afford to lead dummy's queen because if it is covered by a singleton king you will not lose a trick. The advantage of leading the queen comes when the cards lie as in the diagram. If East chooses not to cover, you run the queen and finesse the jack on the next round. If instead East does cover, you win with the ace and see West show out. No problem! You can return to dummy in some other suit and finesse against East's ten.

If you mistakenly begin with a low heart to the jack, there will be no way to recover. East's K-10 will be certain to score a trick.

Lead high to unblock the suit

When you are leading from a hand that contains a doubleton honor it is often right to lead the honor, even if this might cause an enemy trick to be promoted. That's because the honor may block the suit otherwise.

It's time for you to move into the declarer's seat again:

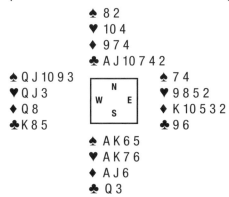

West leads the queen of spades against 3NT and you win with the ace. You will come nowhere near to nine tricks without scoring several club tricks. How do you plan to tackle the suit?

Looking at the clubs in isolation, you would prefer to lead the ♣3 on the first round, collecting all six tricks when West happened to have a singleton king. Leading a low club would be hopeless on the layout shown. Dummy's jack would win the first round but two club tricks would be your limit. If you played the ace next, the king would not fall. If instead you returned to your hand with a heart, West would refuse to cover the queen on the second round of clubs and the suit would be blocked. Of course, you must lead the queen of clubs on the first round. If West declines to cover, the way is now clear for a finesse of the jack on the second round.

Summary

✓ Most of the time it is best to lead a low card to a trick. If the next player contributes an honor for some reason, perhaps because it is bare, he will capture nothing with it. Usually you should lead an honor only if you can afford it to be covered.

✓ When you are leading from a hand that is short of entries, it may be necessary to lead a high card for a finesse even though this will cost a trick against a certain lie of the cards. The purpose is to hold the lead in that hand in order to repeat the finesse.

✓ It is rarely right to lead low to a trick when you hold only a doubleton. By doing so, you may block the suit.

LEAD LOW TO A TRICK

1)

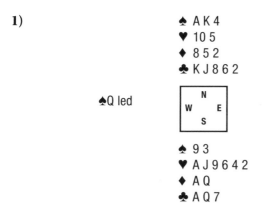

♠ A K 4
♥ 10 5
♦ 8 5 2
♣ K J 8 6 2

♠Q led

♠ 9 3
♥ A J 9 6 4 2
♦ A Q
♣ A Q 7

West leads the ♠Q against your small slam in hearts. After winning with the ace, will you lead the ♥10 or the ♥5? What is the reason for your choice?

2)

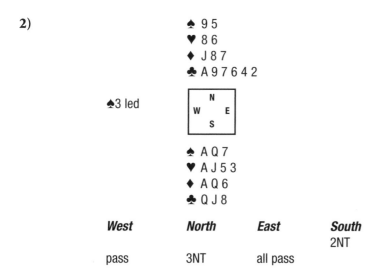

♠ 9 5
♥ 8 6
♦ J 8 7
♣ A 9 7 6 4 2

♠3 led

♠ A Q 7
♥ A J 5 3
♦ A Q 6
♣ Q J 8

West	North	East	South
			2NT
pass	3NT	all pass	

West leads the ♠3 to East's jack and you win with the queen. How will you play the club suit?

ANSWERS

1) You should lead the ♥5, to cater to East holding a singleton king or queen:

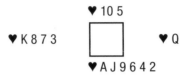

♥ 10 5

♥ K 8 7 3   ♥ Q

♥ A J 9 6 4 2

You capture East's ♥Q with the ace and play low to dummy's ♥10 on the second round. If West refuses to capture, you return to the South hand and lead the ♥J. West will score only one trump trick and you will make the slam.

Suppose you carelessly lead the ♥10 instead. West will make two trump tricks.

2) Leading your lowest club, the eight, would be a poor play. If you rose with dummy's ace, you could never get back to dummy. If instead you ran the eight, you might lost two club tricks. Clearly, you must lead the queen of clubs on the first round. Suppose West covers with the king. What will you do then? (If you have not yet considered this point, go back to look at the problem.)

Since you have four top winners in spades, hearts and diamonds, you need only five club tricks. You should therefore allow West's ♣K to win the trick. This will allow you to score five club tricks when the suit breaks 3-1 or 4-0.

Suppose instead that you had only three winners outside of clubs. You would then need six tricks from the club suit. You would have to win West's ♣K with the ace, return to your hand with the ♣J and (if you were lucky enough to find the suit 2-2) return to dummy by overtaking the ♣8 with the ♣9.

RUN YOUR
⌐LONGEST SUIT⌐

 If you wish to make four tricks in a suit with but three in sight, give the adversaries a chance to discard a card or two before you show your strength. *J.B. Elwell*

When a contract (usually in notrump) seems fairly hopeless, a well-known maxim is: **run your longest suit**. This can gain in two ways. A defender may simply throw the wrong thing, allowing you to score an extra trick in the suit he has unguarded. Another possibility is that a defender may find himself with the sole guard in two or more suits and may be forced to throw away one of his guards.

Let's look at a typical deal on which running the long suit may work well.

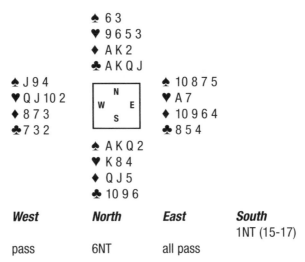

♠ 6 3
♥ 9 6 5 3
♦ A K 2
♣ A K Q J

♠ J 9 4   ♠ 10 8 7 5
♥ Q J 10 2   ♥ A 7
♦ 8 7 3   ♦ 10 9 6 4
♣ 7 3 2   ♣ 8 5 4

♠ A K Q 2
♥ K 8 4
♦ Q J 5
♣ 10 9 6

West	North	East	South
			1NT (15-17)
pass	6NT	all pass	

If you think North's 6NT was an overbid, you're right! West leads the ♥Q to East's ace and a heart is returned. What now?

Prospects may seem rather poor but you can apply pressure on the defenders by running four rounds of clubs. The last club will present East with a tricky decision. He must throw either a spade or a diamond. If he happens to throw a spade, you will score four spade tricks and make your slam.

By changing that last deal slightly we can see how by cashing the winners in your solid suits you may apply genuine pressure on a defender:

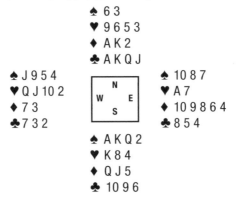

♠ 6 3
♥ 9 6 5 3
♦ A K 2
♣ A K Q J

♠ J 9 5 4   ♠ 10 8 7
♥ Q J 10 2   ♥ A 7
♦ 7 3   ♦ 10 9 8 6 4
♣ 7 3 2   ♣ 8 5 4

♠ A K Q 2
♥ K 8 4
♦ Q J 5
♣ 10 9 6

Again you reach 6NT and West leads the ♥Q to the ace, East returning a heart to your king. When you play off the clubs, throwing a heart from your hand, West can safely release one his two remaining hearts. You then play three rounds of diamonds, ending in the dummy. On the last round West has to find a discard from ♠J-9-5-4 ♥J. If he throws a heart, dummy's ♥9 will be good. If instead he throws a spade, you will make four spade tricks in your hand. West was caught in a 'simple squeeze'. He held the sole guard in both spades and hearts and was forced to throw one of his guards away.

Running the long suit would embarrass you for discards

The time has come to look at a deal or two where it would not be a good idea to run the long suit straight away. On the first of these, running the long suit would put pressure on you rather than on the defenders.

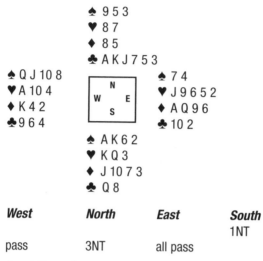

♠ 9 5 3			
♥ 8 7			
♦ 8 5			
♣ A K J 7 5 3			

West	North	East	South
			1NT
pass	3NT	all pass	

West leads the ♠Q and you win immediately, since the defenders could otherwise take four quick tricks in the red suits. What next?

Suppose you blindly decide to follow the guideline 'run your longest suit'. You will not be inconvenienced for your first three discards — you can throw two spades and one heart. When you play the last club you will have to find one further discard from ♠K ♥KQ ♦J1073. In other words you will have to throw one of your guards away! Whatever you throw, you will go down.

It would be poor play to go down in this way. You have eight top tricks in the black suits and can easily establish a ninth trick by leading the ♥K at Trick 2. As soon as you regain the lead you can then take your nine tricks, making the game.

Running the long suit would kill an entry

By this stage in the book you will have realized that there is barely a single guideline in bridge that can be followed without thought. Before playing any contract, you should pause to make a plan. If instead you follow some general advice to 'run the long suit' and pause to make a plan only at Trick 6… you may find that you have blown the contract already. That's what happened when this deal was played:

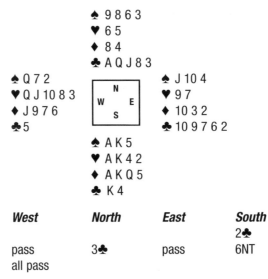

♠ 9 8 6 3
♥ 6 5
♦ 8 4
♣ A Q J 8 3

♠ Q 7 2
♥ Q J 10 8 3
♦ J 9 7 6
♣ 5

N
W　E
S

♠ J 10 4
♥ 9 7
♦ 10 3 2
♣ 10 9 7 6 2

♠ A K 5
♥ A K 4 2
♦ A K Q 5
♣ K 4

West	North	East	South
			2♣
pass	3♣	pass	6NT
all pass			

West led the ♥Q against 6NT and declarer counted five club tricks and seven top cards in the other suits — a total of twelve. Hoping that he might make an overtrick by putting the defenders under pressure, he decided to run his long suit, the clubs. When West showed out on the second round of clubs, declarer realized that he had not in fact started with five club tricks. What was worse, there was now no way to recover and the slam went one down.

The best play at Trick 2, after winning the heart lead, is to play a low spade from both hands. This will set up a twelfth trick immediately if spades happen to break 3-3, as in the diagram. The club suit will then provide an entry to the long spade. If clubs don't behave, and the spades break 4-2 or worse, only one defender will be able to guard the fourth round of spades. You will be able to squeeze him if he holds the sole guard in one of the red suits.

Summary

✓ Playing in a notrump contract you can often put the defenders under real or imagined pressure by running your longest suit.

✓ Do not run the long suit immediately if this will embarrass the hand opposite for discards. Look first for some other way to establish the extra trick(s) you need.

✓ Do not run the long suit immediately when you may need it for entry purposes.

RUN YOUR LONGEST SUIT

1)

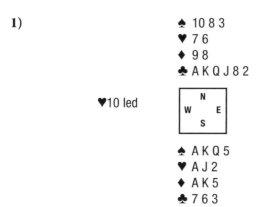

♠ 10 8 3
♥ 7 6
♦ 9 8
♣ A K Q J 8 2

♥10 led

```
      N
  W       E
      S
```

♠ A K Q 5
♥ A J 2
♦ A K 5
♣ 7 6 3

North opens 1♣ and, in macho fashion, you carry the bidding to 7NT. West leads the ♥10 and East plays the queen (obviously from king-queen), which you win with the ace. What chances can you see of making thirteen tricks? Will you run dummy's long suit straight away?

2)

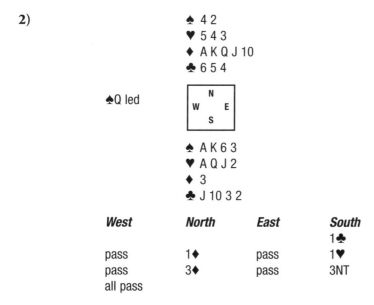

♠ 4 2
♥ 5 4 3
♦ A K Q J 10
♣ 6 5 4

♠Q led

```
      N
  W       E
      S
```

♠ A K 6 3
♥ A Q J 2
♦ 3
♣ J 10 3 2

West	North	East	South
			1♣
pass	1♦	pass	1♥
pass	3♦	pass	3NT
all pass			

West leads the ♠Q against 3NT. How will you play the contract? In particular, will you run dummy's diamonds immediately?

ANSWERS

1) You have twelve top tricks and three solid chances of increasing this to thirteen: (1) spades break 3-3, (2) the ♠J falls in two rounds, (3) East holds four spades and the ♥K and will not be able to keep both guards when you run the clubs.

To take advantage of all these chances you should first cash the ace and king of spades. If the ♠J falls, you will cross to the ♠10 and return to hand with a diamond to score your fourth spade trick. If the ♠J does not fall, you should cash the ace and king of diamonds before running dummy's clubs. When East started with four spades as well as both heart honors the ending will be like this:

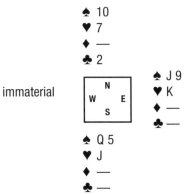

East will have to throw one of his major-suit guards when you play dummy's last club.

2) You should win the spade lead immediately. If you next run the diamonds you will find that you do not have enough safe discards from the South hand. You can afford two spades and one heart. On the last diamond you would have to throw your club guard. You would then go down if a finesse of the ♥Q failed and the defenders could take four club tricks.

You can count eight top tricks and it is easy to bump this to nine by leading the ♥Q before playing on diamonds. You can then win any return and score at least nine tricks.

C H A P T E R **13**

LEAVE THE BIG DECISION UNTIL LAST

 Indecision may tell your adversaries exactly what they are most eager to know. *J.B. Elwell*

Sometimes you can see — the moment the dummy comes down — that the contract will depend on a two-way guess. Perhaps you are missing a queen and will have to decide whether to finesse East or West for that card. Perhaps you hold a doubleton opposite a K-J holding and will have to guess whether to play the jack or the king. When should you make the critical play? Early or late?

The usual advice is to **leave the big decision until last**. That's because it will give you time to gather information about the deal. By playing on other suits first, you may be able to work out each defender's shape and approximate point-count. This is likely to help you with your decision in the key suit.

Let's start with a typical example of declarer performing some detective work, seeking to build up a picture of the entire deal before making a critical queen guess.

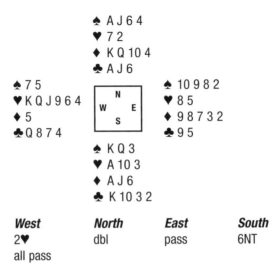

♠ A J 6 4
♥ 7 2
♦ K Q 10 4
♣ A J 6

♠ 7 5
♥ K Q J 9 6 4
♦ 5
♣ Q 8 7 4

♠ 10 9 8 2
♥ 8 5
♦ 9 8 7 3 2
♣ 9 5

♠ K Q 3
♥ A 10 3
♦ A J 6
♣ K 10 3 2

West	North	East	South
2♥	dbl	pass	6NT
all pass			

Impressive leap to 6NT, yes, but can you play the hand to best advantage when West leads the ♥K?

You have eleven top tricks and a successful guess in clubs will bring the total to at least twelve. Suppose you win with the ace of hearts and decide to play on clubs straight away. Which defender should you play for the queen? Since West figures to hold six hearts to his partner's two, East is an initial favorite to hold any missing card, such as the ♣Q, in another suit. You would finesse East for the club queen and in fact go down.

A better idea, after winning with the heart ace, is to play off four rounds in both spades and diamonds, seeking more information. On this deal West would show out on the second diamond and on the third spade. You would then know that his shape was 2-6-1-4. If you had to guess in clubs now you would play West for the ♣Q (because he has four clubs to his partner's two).

In fact an even better play is available, one that makes a certainty of the contract at this stage. If West has retained three of his clubs, his last four cards will be: ♥Q ♣ Q-8-7. You can throw him with a heart and he will have to play a club. You would make the contract even if East had started with a doubleton queen of clubs! You see the benefit of seeking extra information about the distribution? You were able to convert an apparent 50-50 guess into a dead certainty.

Let's look now at some detective work that involves counting the defenders' high-card points.

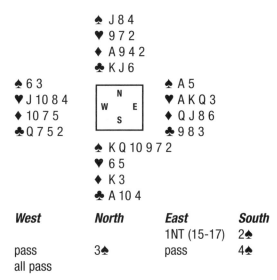

```
                    ♠ J 8 4
                    ♥ 9 7 2
                    ♦ A 9 4 2
                    ♣ K J 6
    ♠ 6 3                           ♠ A 5
    ♥ J 10 8 4          N           ♥ A K Q 3
    ♦ 10 7 5        W       E       ♦ Q J 8 6
    ♣ Q 7 5 2          S           ♣ 9 8 3
                    ♠ K Q 10 9 7 2
                    ♥ 6 5
                    ♦ K 3
                    ♣ A 10 4
```

West	North	East	South
		1NT (15-17)	2♠
pass	3♠	pass	4♠
all pass			

You reach 4♠ and West leads the ♥J. East wins the next heart with the queen and continues with the ♥A. How will you play the contract?

All will depend on guessing which defender holds the ♣Q. If you took the decision immediately — not a wise move — you would play East for the club queen. That's because his 1NT opening promised a high point-count.

A better idea is to seek more information about each defender's point count. You play the ♠K to East's ace and win the trump return with the queen, the suit breaking 2-2. East has shown up with thirteen points in the major suits so far. It's time to see what he has in diamonds! You play the king and ace of diamonds and ruff a diamond, the jack appearing from East. Returning to dummy with a trump, you lead the last diamond. All depends on who produces the ♦Q. When the cards lie as in the diagram, the queen will appear from East. He has shown up with 16 points already, so cannot hold the ♣Q. You will finesse clubs through West.

Suppose that West had been dealt the diamond queen. East would then hold only 14 points outside clubs and would be marked with the ♣Q. By counting the defenders' points, you would avoid a guess in either case.

Playing the key suit early applies pressure

Perhaps you were so impressed by the previous two deals (go on, admit it!) that you think detective work is always a good idea. No, there are some deals, particularly at the six-level, where you will make life very easy for the defenders if you play the other suits first. To apply pressure, you must lead the key suit early — when the defenders are not expecting it:

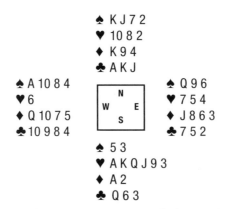

♠ K J 7 2
♥ 10 8 2
♦ K 9 4
♣ A K J

♠ A 10 8 4
♥ 6
♦ Q 10 7 5
♣ 10 9 8 4

♠ Q 9 6
♥ 7 5 4
♦ J 8 6 3
♣ 7 5 2

♠ 5 3
♥ A K Q J 9 3
♦ A 2
♣ Q 6 3

West leads the ♣10 against your small slam in hearts and all will depend on your spade guess. Does West hold the ♠A or the ♠Q? Should you try to get some further information on the hand?

Suppose you draw trumps and play off the club and diamond winners, ruffing the third round of diamonds. You will make it entirely obvious that you are solid outside spades. Since West knows that his side must take two spade tricks to beat the slam, there is no chance at all that he will rise with the ace when you lead a spade towards dummy.

Now try something different. Win the club lead with the queen and immediately lead a spade from your hand! Many Wests will be caught napping. Expecting you to draw trumps first, they will not be prepared for a play on spades. Nor may it be obvious whether they should rise with the ace. If you have a singleton spade, and perhaps an inevitable loser in the trump suit, it would be right to do so. Many, many Wests will give the position away, either rising with the ace or thinking about it. In the absence of any such reaction you will play West for the queen instead.

Summary

✓ It is usually right to seek information on the defenders' hands (their shape and their point-count) before taking a key decision.

✓ At the small slam level you can put pressure on a defender by leading towards a king in dummy at a very early stage.

LEAVE THE BIG DECISION UNTIL LAST

1)

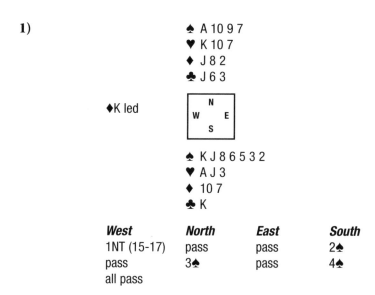

♠ A 10 9 7
♥ K 10 7
♦ J 8 2
♣ J 6 3

♦K led

♠ K J 8 6 5 3 2
♥ A J 3
♦ 10 7
♣ K

West	North	East	South
1NT (15-17)	pass	pass	2♠
pass	3♠	pass	4♠
all pass			

West opens the defense with the ♦ K-A followed by a diamond to his partner's queen. You ruff the third round and draw trumps, finding that West has the expected doubleton queen. How will you continue the play?

2)

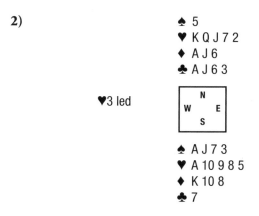

♠ 5
♥ K Q J 7 2
♦ A J 6
♣ A J 6 3

♥3 led

♠ A J 7 3
♥ A 10 9 8 5
♦ K 10 8
♣ 7

Someone makes a mistake in the bidding and you reach a grand slam in hearts. West leads a trump, the suit breaking 2-1, and you are relieved to see that there is fair play for the contract. However, unless you can ruff out K-Q-x in one of the black suits, you will have to guess the diamonds. What is your plan to maximize your prospects of picking up the ♦Q?

ANSWERS

1) It may seem that you need to guess who holds the ♥Q but it would be poor play to tackle the hearts directly. Instead you should lead the ♣K. When West wins with the ace he cannot safely play on diamonds (this would give you a ruff-and-discard) or hearts (this would save you a guess). If he tries to cash the ♣Q, you can ruff and dummy's ♣J will be set up. So, the only apparently troublesome play from West will be a low club, with dummy's jack losing to East's queen. The contract is now yours for the taking! Do you see why? West will have shown up with only thirteen points outside hearts. To make up the fifteen he needs for a 1NT opening he must hold the ♥Q. You will therefore finesse him for that card.

2) After drawing the outstanding trump you should ruff three rounds of both black suits. This will give you a complete count on the defenders' hands. Suppose the cards lie like this:

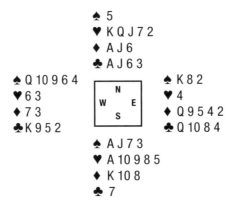

East discarded on the second trump and subsequently showed up with three spades and four clubs. So he holds five diamonds to his partner's two. That makes him a 5-2 favorite to hold the diamond queen! You play the ♦A and finesse through East. On this occasion the favorite romps home and you make your grand. Well bid, partner! Even if the diamonds proved to be 4-3, one way or other, you would bend the odds significantly in your favor by playing the defender who started with four diamonds for the queen.

THIRD HAND HIGH

When you are trying to win the trick, play high third in hand.
J.B. Elwell.

One of the first 'rules' impressed on defenders is that you should always play high in the third seat. The reason why this is usually a good idea is plain to see:

You are sitting East and partner leads the ♠2. If you play 'third hand high', rising with the ace, your side will score the first three tricks in the suit. In no-trump you will score a fourth spade trick too. Suppose you ignored the guide-line and played the ten on the first round instead of the ace. Declarer would then score an undeserved trick with the queen.

This situation is similar:

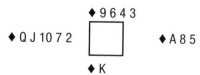

When partner leads the ♦Q against a contract such as 4♠, you must overtake with the ace. If you fail to do so, declarer will score a trick with the king and you will never make your ace.

Even when you cannot win the trick it is still normally best to play high. By doing so you hope to set up lower cards in your hand or in partner's:

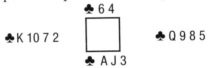

               ♣ 6 4

♣ K 10 7 2   ♣ Q 9 8 5

               ♣ A J 3

Partner leads the ♣2, against some major-suit contract. Your queen forces declarer's ace and partner's king can then beat the jack on the second round of the suit. If you do not play the queen, declarer will give an amused shake of the head and win two tricks with the jack and the ace.

This is all fairly basic stuff, of course. The basic purpose of playing 'third hand high' is clear. You play high in an attempt to win the trick. By doing so you prevent declarer from winning the trick with a lesser card.

It's time to see the situations, and there are many of them, where you must break the general guideline of 'third hand high'.

Do not play high when you can finesse against the dummy

If you cast your eye back to the previous three diagrams you will see that dummy always contained low cards. When dummy has an honor, this may affect your play in the third seat.

               ♦ Q 7 5

♦ K 9 6 3   ♦ A J 8 2

               ♦ 10 4

Partner leads the ♦3 — against 3NT, let's say — and declarer plays low from dummy. If you play the ace ('third hand high') declarer will eventually score a trick with the queen. Play the jack instead, keeping your ace to deal with dummy's queen, and you will fare better. The jack will win and you will be able to run four diamond tricks.

Such a play, inserting the jack, is known as finessing against the dummy. In a way it is easier than the sort of finesses that declarer may take. You can actually see the queen that you are finessing against!

The same play may work well even if declarer holds the king of diamonds instead of your partner:

               ♦ Q 7 5

♦ 10 9 6 3   ♦ A J 8 2

               ♦ K 4

Once again your partner leads the ♦3 against 3NT, declarer playing low from the dummy. If you rise with the ace declarer will score two tricks, one with the king and another with the queen. Play the jack, as before, and you restrict him to one trick.

Sometimes the situation is not so clear-cut. Look at this awkward situation:

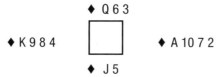

```
                    ♦ Q 6 3
    ♦ K 9 8 4                      ♦ A 10 7 2
                    ♦ J 5
```

Partner leads the ♦4, dummy playing low. Should you play the ace or not?

In notrump you cannot lose by playing the ten, retaining the ace over dummy's queen. If declarer has the jack, he will score one diamond trick whatever you do. But suppose that declarer is in a major-suit contract. Now it may be essential for the defense to score two diamond tricks. The cards may lie like this:

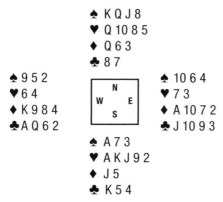

```
                    ♠ K Q J 8
                    ♥ Q 10 8 5
                    ♦ Q 6 3
                    ♣ 8 7
    ♠ 9 5 2                       ♠ 10 6 4
    ♥ 6 4              N           ♥ 7 3
    ♦ K 9 8 4       W   E         ♦ A 10 7 2
    ♣ A Q 6 2          S          ♣ J 10 9 3
                    ♠ A 7 3
                    ♥ A K J 9 2
                    ♦ J 5
                    ♣ K 5 4
```

South arrives in a heart game and your partner leads the ♦4, the only lead to give the defenders a chance. To beat the game you must rise with the diamond ace and switch to a club. Your side will then score two diamonds and two clubs.

Do you see why it is a 'guess' whether or not to rise with the diamond ace? Firstly partner might hold precisely ♦K-J-4. In that case you could score three tricks in the diamond suit, by playing the ten on the first trick. Secondly partner might have led from something like ♦J-8-5-4. In that case rising with the ace would give declarer two diamond tricks.

In such situations you must try to judge what is the best chance to beat the contract. Even if declarer does hold the ♦K, best defense may be to rise with the ace and switch to the ♣J. You hope to score one diamond, two clubs and a further trick in one of the red suits.

Do not play high when this would break communications

When you have bid a suit and partner subsequently leads that suit against a no-trump contract, playing 'third hand high' may break communications between the defenders. Take the East cards here:

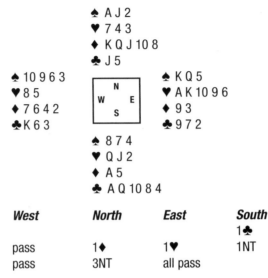

	North	East	South
West			1♣
pass	1♦	1♥	1NT
pass	3NT	all pass	

You overcall in hearts and partner leads the ♥8 against 3NT. Let's see what happens first if you play 'third hand high', winning with the king. Whether you play the ace of hearts next or a low heart, the contract will succeed. When declarer takes a losing finesse in clubs, your partner will have no heart to return.

Instead you should play the ♥9 on the first round, forcing declarer to take his heart trick immediately. The contract now goes down. When your partner wins the ♣K he will have a heart left. You will then score four heart tricks and one club trick.

There are many such situations where flouting the 'third hand high' rule will assist your communications.

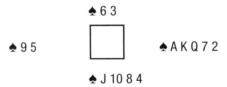

You have overcalled in spades and partner leads the ♠9 against 3NT. Play low, forcing out declarer's stopper, and you will beat the contract whenever partner can gain the lead before declarer can cash nine tricks. Play high and communication with partner will be lost.

On the next deal, declarer has a double stopper in the suit that you have bid, as East. It is essential to knock out one of declarer's stoppers while partner still has a card left in your suit.

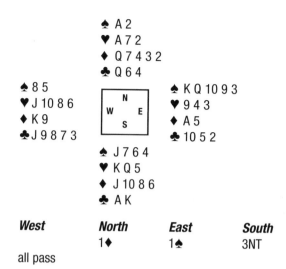

```
                    ♠ A 2
                    ♥ A 7 2
                    ♦ Q 7 4 3 2
                    ♣ Q 6 4
   ♠ 8 5                              ♠ K Q 10 9 3
   ♥ J 10 8 6      N                  ♥ 9 4 3
   ♦ K 9       W       E              ♦ A 5
   ♣ J 9 8 7 3      S                 ♣ 10 5 2
                    ♠ J 7 6 4
                    ♥ K Q 5
                    ♦ J 10 8 6
                    ♣ A K
```

West	North	East	South
	1♦	1♠	3NT

all pass

You don't like South's 3NT bid? Perhaps not, but we can't waste time discussing the bidding. How would you defend in the East seat when partner leads the ♠8 and declarer plays low from the dummy?

Suppose you 'play high in third seat', winning with the queen. Declarer will win the next round of spades with dummy's ace and play on diamonds. When your partner wins with the king he will have no spade to return. The contract will easily be made.

It is obvious from the bidding that declarer has a second stopper in the spade suit. You must aim to remove this at Trick 1, while your partner still has a spade left. Instead of winning with the spade queen, you should play the nine of spades, forcing declarer's jack. Now you're in business! When declarer plays on diamonds your partner will win the king and play his remaining spade to dislodge dummy's ace. You win the next round of diamonds and can then cash three spade tricks to defeat the contract.

BY THE WAY

Suppose your spades in the East seat had been slightly weaker: K-J-10-9-3 against South's Q-7-6-4. Do you think that a similar defense (playing the nine at Trick 1) would have succeeded? It would if declarer won the first trick with the queen. Once again your partner could have cleared the spades when he won the ♦K. However, a skilled declarer would allow your ♠9 to win! It would do you no good to play a low spade to dummy's bare ace next because South would still have a second stopper.

Play low to maintain communications for a ruff

When partner leads a doubleton against a trump contract and you hold the ace of that suit but no other entry, it may pay you to withhold the ace at Trick 1. You hope that your partner holds a top trump and will be able to cross to your hand later for a ruff. Take the East cards again here:

```
                    ♠ 9 6 5
                    ♥ 10 4 3
                    ♦ A K
                    ♣ A J 9 8 5
    ♠ A Q 3                        ♠ 8
    ♥ 9 7          N               ♥ A J 8 6 5
    ♦ Q 10 8 6 2   W   E           ♦ 9 7 4 3
    ♣ 10 6 4          S            ♣ Q 7 2
                    ♠ K J 10 7 4 2
                    ♥ K Q 2
                    ♦ J 5
                    ♣ K 3
```

West	North	East	South
			1♠
pass	2♣	pass	2♠
pass	4♠	all pass	

BY THE WAY

Suppose you cannot figure out whether partner's lead is a singleton or a doubleton. Should you hold up your ace or not? It is usually better to assume a singleton, since this is a much more attractive opening lead.

Your partner leads the ♥9. How do you read this card? Do you think it could be a singleton?

If West holds only one heart, this would leave South with four hearts. He would then surely have rebid 2♥ rather than 2♠. You should therefore play partner for a doubleton heart. Do not play your ace of hearts at Trick 1. Keep it for later! Follow with an encouraging card (whichever spot card fits your signaling method).

Declarer wins the heart lead, crosses to dummy with a diamond and plays a trump to the jack and queen. Because you have retained the ace of hearts your partner can now cross to your hand and receive a heart ruff. The spade game will go one down.

Play low to avoid setting up tricks for declarer

When partner's opening lead is from spot cards and you hold the ace in third seat, you can sometimes tell that playing the ace will assist declarer. It will set up winners in his hand. By refusing to play the ace, even sometimes sacrificing it, you may save your side a trick. Take the East cards here:

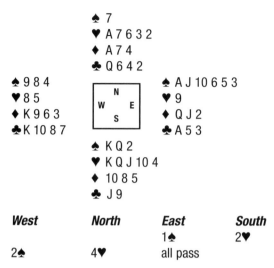

♠ 7
♥ A 7 6 3 2
♦ A 7 4
♣ Q 6 4 2

♠ 9 8 4
♥ 8 5
♦ K 9 6 3
♣ K 10 8 7

N
W E
S

♠ A J 10 6 5 3
♥ 9
♦ Q J 2
♣ A 5 3

♠ K Q 2
♥ K Q J 10 4
♦ 10 8 5
♣ J 9

West	North	East	South
		1♠	2♥
2♠	4♥	all pass	

South arrives in four hearts and West leads the ♠9 (lead high from three small in partner's suit when you have raised). How will you defend with the East cards?

Partner's lead tells you that South holds ♠K-Q-x-x or ♠K-Q-x. If you rise with the ace of spades, you will set up two spade tricks for declarer and this will allow him to discard both of dummy's diamond losers. It is hard to see how the contract could be defeated after such a start and you do best to play the ten of spades instead.

If declarer looks pleased to have avoided a spade loser, the smile will soon leave his face. He has no way to avoid two diamond losers and two club losers and will now go one down. Had you risen with the spade ace, ten tricks would have been easy.

When we come to look at 'second hand low' in Chapter 17, we will see that you should be wary of rising with an ace when declarer leads a side-suit singleton from dummy. As we have just seen, the same situation can arise when partner leads the suit and there is a singleton in dummy.

Summary

✓ The basis of the guideline 'third hand high' is that you should attempt to win the trick or at least drive out a high card from declarer.

✓ When playing your highest card will set up an honor in dummy, consider playing your second best card if it is the nine or higher.

✓ When partner leads your long suit, defending a notrump contract, consider retaining your high cards to preserve communications. For example with A-K-x-x-x, playing low will drive out one of declarer's stoppers. It may also leave partner with a card to play in the suit, should he gain the lead.

✓ When partner leads a short suit, seeking a ruff, consider holding up an ace in the suit when you judge that the lead may be a doubleton and you have no other entry.

THIRD HAND HIGH

1)

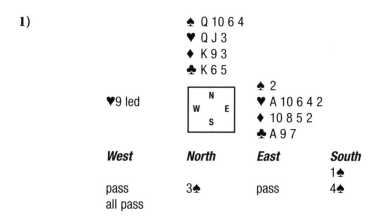

♠ Q 10 6 4
♥ Q J 3
♦ K 9 3
♣ K 6 5

♥9 led

♠ 2
♥ A 10 6 4 2
♦ 10 8 5 2
♣ A 9 7

West	North	East	South
			1♠
pass	3♠	pass	4♠
all pass			

Your partner leads the ♥9 against South's game in spades. Will you hold up the ace of hearts or not? What is your general plan for the defense?

2)

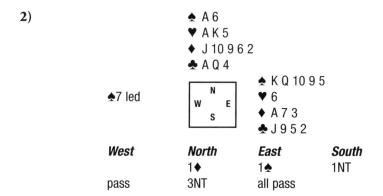

♠ A 6
♥ A K 5
♦ J 10 9 6 2
♣ A Q 4

♠7 led

♠ K Q 10 9 5
♥ 6
♦ A 7 3
♣ J 9 5 2

West	North	East	South
	1♦	1♠	1NT
pass	3NT	all pass	

Partner leads the ♠7 against 3NT and declarer plays low from dummy. Which card will you play? What is the reason for your choice?

ANSWERS

1) You should not hold up the ♥A. The purpose of such a hold-up is to maintain communications. Since you hold the ♣A as an entry, communications are of no concern. You should win with the ♥A and return the ♥2, your lowest spot-card, to suggest a club return.

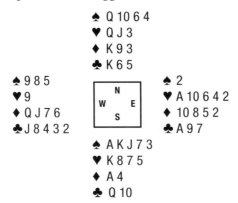

A heart to the ace, heart ruff, a club to the ace, heart ruff. One down before declarer has time to blink!

2) It is clear that South holds at least jack fourth in the spade suit. The full deal may be:

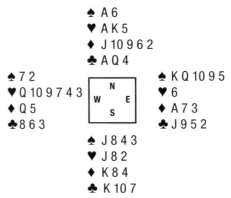

To beat 3NT you must overtake partner's ♠7 with the nine, forcing South's jack. When partner gains the lead with the ♦Q he will clear the spades for one down. If you play the king or queen of spades at Trick 1, West will have no spade to play when he gains the lead in diamonds.

RETURN PARTNER'S SUIT

 To return partner's lead, or not? At times you will find this a most difficult question to decide. *J.B. Elwell*

The guideline **always return partner's suit** applies mainly in notrump contracts, which are often a race between the two sides. Can the defenders set up enough tricks to beat the contract before declarer sets up enough to make it? When the opening lead has already removed one of declarer's stoppers, it usually makes good sense to pursue that suit, rather than start afresh elsewhere.

Take the East cards on this typical deal:

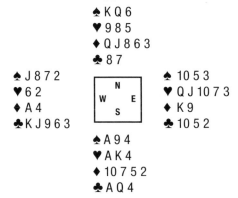

♠ K Q 6
♥ 9 8 5
♦ Q J 8 6 3
♣ 8 7

♠ J 8 7 2   ♠ 10 5 3
♥ 6 2   ♥ Q J 10 7 3
♦ A 4   ♦ K 9
♣ K J 9 6 3   ♣ 10 5 2

♠ A 9 4
♥ A K 4
♦ 10 7 5 2
♣ A Q 4

Your partner leads the ♣6 against 3NT and your ten is won by South's queen. Declarer now plays a diamond to the queen and your king. Should you switch to a heart or continue partner's suit?

The job of knocking out declarer's club stoppers is already half done. Complete it, by returning a club, and the contract will go down. Partner will win the next round of diamonds and cash his established club tricks. If you switch to hearts instead, declarer will make the contract easily. Even if you found partner with a doubleton heart honor (the most you could reasonably expect), a heart switch would not be productive. You would have no entry left to your hand.

Look back at the diagram and imagine North is playing in 3NT. You lead the ♥Q and declarer wins with the ace. When he plays on diamonds, your partner should rise with the ace and return your suit. Again you would beat the contract by persevering with the suit that has been led.

However, you need your wits about you, when defending, and there are various situations when returning partner's suit will not be the best idea. Let's see some of them.

Switch because there is no future in partner's suit

Sometimes you can tell from the play at Trick 1 that declarer has partner's suit well stopped and will make the contract if you continue to plug away in that direction. Take the East cards here:

```
                    ♠ K Q J 6
                    ♥ 9 8 5
                    ♦ K 10 9 3
                    ♣ 7 5
  ♠ 9 7 3            ┌─────────┐        ♠ 10 8 5 2
  ♥ J 6 4            │    N    │        ♥ A Q 7 2
  ♦ 6 5              │  W   E  │        ♦ A Q 4
  ♣ Q 9 8 3 2        │    S    │        ♣ 10 4
                     └─────────┘
                    ♠ A 4
                    ♥ K 10 3
                    ♦ J 8 7 2
                    ♣ A K J 6
```

West	North	East	South
			1NT (15-17)
pass	2♣	pass	2♦
pass	3NT	all pass	

Partner leads the ♣3 and declarer wins your ten with the jack. He next runs the ♦8 to your queen. How do you assess the situation?

Many defenders would return partner's suit here, playing the ♣4. There's not much point in it. Even if partner's clubs are quite strong and can be set up, he will have no entry to enjoy them. You are the one looking at the two red aces and you know from South's opening bid that your partner cannot hold much in the way of high cards.

A better idea is to switch to hearts. You know from South's Stayman response that he cannot hold more than three hearts. If partner holds the ♥J, or if South holds ♥K-J doubleton, you can set up the suit. Declarer is not a happy camper when he sees your ♥2 on the table. However he plays, the defenders will score three hearts and two diamonds. One down!

Switch because you need tricks from more than one suit

When partner's suit has already been established, it is not always right for you to return that suit when you gain the lead. If you need tricks from another suit too, in order to beat the contract, you may have to play on that suit instead. Take the East cards on this deal:

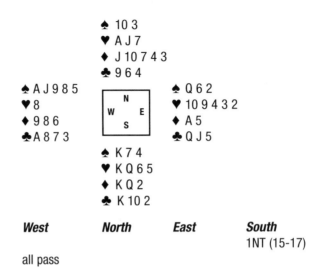

	♠ 10 3		
	♥ A J 7		
	♦ J 10 7 4 3		
	♣ 9 6 4		

♠ A J 9 8 5   ♠ Q 6 2
♥ 8   ♥ 10 9 4 3 2
♦ 9 8 6   ♦ A 5
♣ A 8 7 3   ♣ Q J 5

	♠ K 7 4		
	♥ K Q 6 5		
	♦ K Q 2		
	♣ K 10 2		

West	*North*	*East*	*South*
			1NT (15-17)

all pass

West leads a fourth-best ♠8 against South's contract of 1NT. You play the queen and this forces the king. Declarer plays on diamonds now, leading the king and continuing with the queen if you choose to duck the first round. What should you do next?

If you apply the Rule of Eleven to partner's opening lead, you can deduce that declarer started with only one card higher than the eight. (You subtract the value of the card led, 8 in this example, from 11. The answer is 3 and that is the number of cards higher than the eight that are held by North, East and South. You can see two of the three higher cards, dummy's ten and your queen, so declarer must hold just one — the king that he has already played.) It follows that partner's spades are ready to run. But even if he has led from a six-card suit, this will give the defense only six tricks — five spades and the diamond ace. You therefore need at least one more trick, probably two, to beat the contract.

The heart situation does not look at all promising and your best move is to switch to the queen of clubs. Partner has the ace sitting over South's king on this occasion. So, a switch to the ♣Q will beat the contract, giving you four spade tricks, two clubs and the ♦A. If instead you woodenly return partner's suit, he will score four tricks there but will not be able to attack clubs from his side of the table. Another fish will have escaped your net!

Switch to receive a signal from partner

When there is a long and strong suit in the dummy which will give declarer all the tricks he needs, you have to cash out quickly. If you try to take a trick in a suit where declarer has a winner, or is void and can ruff, you can wave goodbye to any remaining winners that you might have cashed. In such a situation you must be wary of returning partner's suit without thought. Look at this deal from East's point of view:

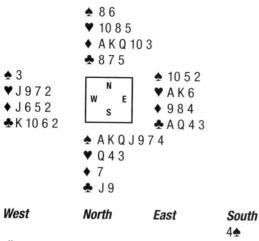

```
                    ♠ 8 6
                    ♥ 10 8 5
                    ♦ A K Q 10 3
                    ♣ 8 7 5
    ♠ 3                           ♠ 10 5 2
    ♥ J 9 7 2       ┌─────────┐   ♥ A K 6
    ♦ J 6 5 2       │   N     │   ♦ 9 8 4
    ♣ K 10 6 2      │ W   E   │   ♣ A Q 4 3
                    │   S     │
                    └─────────┘
                    ♠ A K Q J 9 7 4
                    ♥ Q 4 3
                    ♦ 7
                    ♣ J 9
```

West	North	East	South
			4♠

all pass

Your partner, who apparently belongs to the 'never lead from a king' school, places the ♥2 on the table. You score two tricks with the king and ace and must now decide what to do next. Any ideas?

It is entirely possible that your partner has led from queen fourth and that you have a third trick to take from the heart suit. Playing another heart now would be poor defense, though. Do you see why? Even if partner does have the queen of hearts you will still need a fourth trick to beat the spade game. So, you might as well play the ace of clubs first, before committing yourself to any decision. The advantage of this move is that partner can give you a signal — playing a high club to encourage a club continuation, a low club to request a return to hearts.

When the cards lie as in the diagram, partner will give you the ten of clubs. A second club will then defeat the game. If instead partner held the queen of hearts and only the queen or jack of clubs, he would discourage clubs by playing his lowest card in the suit. You would then play a third heart.

BY THE WAY

Suppose, on this deal, that East held slightly better clubs: A-K-4-3. How could he discover if both clubs would stand up? He would lead the king of clubs. The lead of an ace in this situation asks for an attitude signal (high to encourage, low to discourage). The lead of a king asks instead for a count signal (high with an even number of cards in the suit, low with an odd number). If West were to signal high on the king of clubs, East would know that West held four clubs and South had two. He would know that a second club would stand up. If instead West showed an odd number of clubs, this would strongly suggest that declarer held a singleton club. East would then play a third heart instead, hoping partner held the queen.

Switch to knock out an entry to dummy

Even when partner's suit does offer some promise, you may find that the most urgent task before you is to kill a key entry to dummy. Suppose you had been East here. Would you have seen what to do?

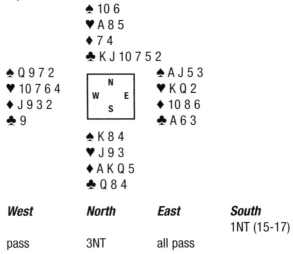

♠ 10 6
♥ A 8 5
♦ 7 4
♣ K J 10 7 5 2

♠ Q 9 7 2
♥ 10 7 6 4
♦ J 9 3 2
♣ 9

♠ A J 5 3
♥ K Q 2
♦ 10 8 6
♣ A 6 3

♠ K 8 4
♥ J 9 3
♦ A K Q 5
♣ Q 8 4

West	North	East	South
			1NT (15-17)
pass	3NT	all pass	

Partner leads the ♠2 to your ace. What will you return?

Let's see first what happens if you return partner's suit, playing back the ♠3. Declarer knows from the lead that spades are 4-4. He will rise with the ♠K and clear the club suit. It won't help you to hold up the club ace for a couple of rounds because dummy's ♥A will be an entry to the good clubs. Once you have scored three spades and the club ace, declarer will step in and claim the remainder.

To beat 3NT you must kill dummy's clubs by removing the heart entry. At Trick 2 you should switch to the ♥K. If declarer allows this to win, you will switch back to spades, setting up five tricks for the defense.

The same sort of continue-or-switch decision may be required in a suit contract. Try your luck with the East cards on the next deal:

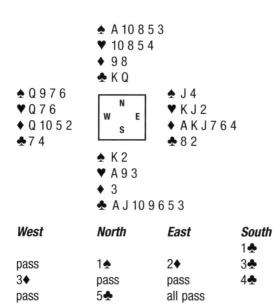

♠ A 10 8 5 3
♥ 10 8 5 4
♦ 9 8
♣ K Q

♠ Q 9 7 6
♥ Q 7 6
♦ Q 10 5 2
♣ 7 4

♠ J 4
♥ K J 2
♦ A K J 7 6 4
♣ 8 2

♠ K 2
♥ A 9 3
♦ 3
♣ A J 10 9 6 5 3

West	North	East	South
			1♣
pass	1♠	2♦	3♣
3♦	pass	pass	4♣
pass	5♣	all pass	

Partner leads the ♦2 to your king. What should you do next?

Perhaps partner raised you with only three-card support and another diamond will stand up. It is also possible that declarer has some losing hearts in his hand. However, the only way he can dispose of any losers is by setting up dummy's spade suit. To prevent this from happening, you should switch to a trump, removing a key entry to dummy.

Let's see what happens if you return a heart or a diamond. Declarer will win the trick, play the king and ace of spades and ruff a spade. He will then cross to a trump honor and ruff the last spade good. A trump to dummy's remaining honor will draw the defenders' trumps and he will discard one of his heart losers on the long spade. After a trump switch at Trick 2, declarer does not have enough entries for this play.

Summary

✓ The reason why it is often a good idea to return partner's suit, when defending a notrump contract, is that the opening lead will already have removed one of declarer's stoppers.

✓ Sometimes you can tell that a continuation of partner's suit will not beat the contract. A switch elsewhere may provide better prospects.

✓ When dummy contains a long suit, look for a switch that may remove a key entry to dummy, killing the suit.

RETURN PARTNER'S SUIT

NOW TRY THESE...

1)

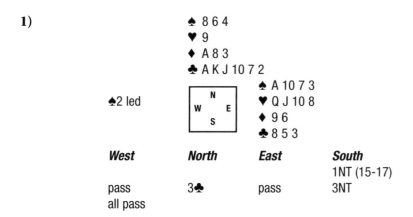

♠ 8 6 4
♥ 9
♦ A 8 3
♣ A K J 10 7 2

♠2 led

♠ A 10 7 3
♥ Q J 10 8
♦ 9 6
♣ 8 5 3

West	North	East	South
			1NT (15-17)
pass	3♣	pass	3NT
all pass			

Partner leads a fourth-best ♠2 to your ace, the jack appearing from South. What will you do next? What does partner need to hold to allow you to beat the contract?

2)

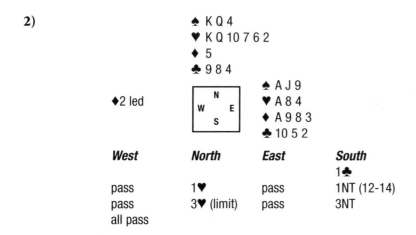

♠ K Q 4
♥ K Q 10 7 6 2
♦ 5
♣ 9 8 4

♦2 led

♠ A J 9
♥ A 8 4
♦ A 9 8 3
♣ 10 5 2

West	North	East	South
			1♣
pass	1♥	pass	1NT (12-14)
pass	3♥ (limit)	pass	3NT
all pass			

Partner leads the ♦2 to your ace. What card will you return?

ANSWERS

1) It is possible that partner holds king-fourth in the spade suit. However, this will not be good enough to beat the contract. You can see 19 points in your hand and the dummy. Add in declarer's minimum of 15 points and that leaves your partner with at most a six-count. If three of partner's points are in spades, declarer would be marked with the ♥A and at least one red-suit king, giving him enough tricks to make his game.

   The only real chance of beating the contract is to find partner with the ace of hearts. If he does, then unless South has opened 1NT with a five-card heart suit, your partner will hold ace-fourth in hearts. A switch to the ♥Q will net four more tricks for the defense.

2) If your partner's diamonds are reasonably strong, you will beat the contract by returning his suit. This is risky, though, and will allow the game to make if this is the layout:

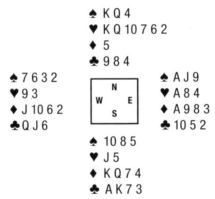

```
                    ♠ K Q 4
                    ♥ K Q 10 7 6 2
                    ♦ 5
                    ♣ 9 8 4
     ♠ 7 6 3 2                      ♠ A J 9
     ♥ 9 3          ┌─────────┐     ♥ A 8 4
     ♦ J 10 6 2     │    N    │     ♦ A 9 8 3
     ♣ Q J 6        │ W     E │     ♣ 10 5 2
                    │    S    │
                    └─────────┘
                    ♠ 10 8 5
                    ♥ J 5
                    ♦ K Q 7 4
                    ♣ A K 7 3
```

   A much surer defense is to return the ♠J! This will kill the entry to dummy's heart suit. (Declarer cannot duck effectively because you will continue with ace and another spade.) You will subsequently hold up the ace of hearts for one round, leaving declarer well short of his target.

C H A P T E R 16

COVER AN HONOR WITH AN HONOR

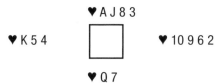

 It is astounding how difficult one finds it not to cover an honor led. *J.B. Elwell*

One of the most famous guidelines given to fledgling defenders is: **cover an honor with an honor**. You may be surprised to hear that this is often very poor advice! If each of your friends gave you a dollar every time they lost a trick by covering an honor incorrectly, you would soon be buying a yacht and a larger house.

Let's see first why covering can sometimes be a good idea. The general purpose is to promote a lesser card, either in your own hand or in your partner's. Look at this position:

♥ A J 8 3

♥ K 5 4   □   ♥ 10 9 6 2

♥ Q 7

You are sitting West and declarer leads the queen on the first round of hearts. Let's suppose that you fail to cover. The queen will win and declarer will subsequently finesse the jack successfully, scoring three heart tricks. If you cover with the king, forcing dummy's ace, three big cards are consumed on one trick. Your partner's ten and nine grow in stature and will prevent declarer from scoring more than two tricks.

The purpose of covering an honor is clear, then. You do so to promote the value of lesser cards, either in your own hand or partner's. Let's see some more situations where a cover will gain a trick.

Suppose declarer leads the ♣10 (we will see in a moment that he is not very likely to do this). If you fail to cover, the ten will be run to East's queen. A subsequent finesse of the jack will succeed and declarer will score three club tricks. Cover the ten with the king and declarer will make only two club tricks. Your partner's Q-9 will be promoted in value.

Sometimes you need to cover cards that are below honor rank:

If you let South's ♦9 run to partner's queen, declarer can finesse the jack successfully on the next round. Cover the nine with the ten and there will be no way for him to score more than one trick.

So far, covering has seemed like a good idea, but the time has arrived to look at the many occasions where covering may cost a trick.

Covering saves declarer a guess

Declarer will often lead an honor in the hope that he can save himself a guess by tempting a cover. Suppose you are West here:

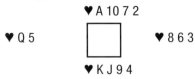

South has a two-way guess in the heart suit. Putting you to the test, he may well lead the ♥J from his hand. If you blindly follow the 'cover an honor with an honor' guideline, you will spare him a guess. Suppose instead that you are a cool customer, familiar with the situation. You will play low smoothly when the ♥J appears. Declarer is then likely to place your partner with the missing queen. He will win the first round with dummy's ace and play low to the nine on the next round. Your queen will make a trick!

Perhaps you would be nervous that this was the lie of the heart suit:

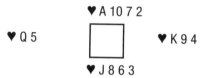

♥ A 10 7 2

♥ Q 5　　　□　　　♥ K 9 4

♥ J 8 6 3

Now you would need to cover the ♥J to promote two tricks for partner's K-9. It may seem that you cannot tell which of these holdings declarer has and that it is therefore a complete guess whether to cover. That is not true, in fact. Do you see why?

When declarer holds J-8-6-3, as in the last diagram, he would not lead the jack. He would lead low to the ten, picking up the suit for one loser on this lay-out against any defense! So, when the jack is led you should play low smoothly, assuming that declarer has a guess in the suit. A sound declarer will rarely lead an honor unless he can afford it to be covered. You should therefore be reluctant to cover unless you have a good reason.

Covering helps declarer choose between two lines of play

Sometimes declarer has a choice of two lines. When the defenders can be relied on to cover any honor, he may be able to combine the two chances.

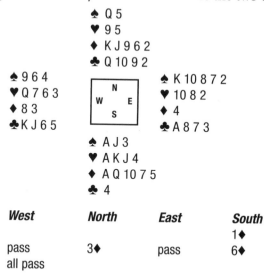

♠ Q 5
♥ 9 5
♦ K J 9 6 2
♣ Q 10 9 2

♠ 9 6 4　　　　　　　　♠ K 10 8 7 2
♥ Q 7 6 3　　　　　　　♥ 10 8 2
♦ 8 3　　　　　　　　　♦ 4
♣ K J 6 5　　　　　　　♣ A 8 7 3

♠ A J 3
♥ A K J 4
♦ A Q 10 7 5
♣ 4

West	North	East	South
			1♦
pass	3♦	pass	6♦
all pass			

West leads the ♣5 against the diamond slam and East beats dummy's nine with the ace. Declarer ruffs the club return and crosses to dummy with the king of trumps. What now? If East holds the spade king, a successful finesse in the suit will yield the contract; the three remaining losers in the majors can all be ruffed in the dummy. If instead East holds the queen of hearts, it will work better to finesse in hearts. A spade can then be thrown from dummy and again twelve tricks will result.

It may seem that declarer has to guess which finesse to take. Not against 90% of the world's defenders! Suppose declarer leads the ♠Q from dummy at Trick 3. Most defenders holding those East cards will shrug their shoulders and cover with the king. The slam will then be made. Think what will happen if East is clever enough not to cover. Declarer will surely place the king of spades with West. In that case he will rise with the ace of spades, return to dummy with a second round of trump, and take the heart finesse instead. One down!

To become one of the world's top 10% of defenders, beating such contracts, you must visualize declarer's hand and calculate what options, or problems, he may have. Here it is clear from the bidding that South must hold the ace and king of hearts. The contract can be beaten only if he has a choice of finesses to take in the major suits.

Covering establishes a second-round finesse

There is another frequent situation where covering an honor can cost a trick. What do you make of this position, viewed from the East seat?

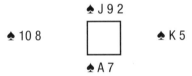

Declarer leads the ♠Q from dummy. If you cover with the king, declarer can win with the ace and finesse the nine on the next round. He will score four spade tricks. Suppose instead that you refuse to cover. The queen will win and these cards will remain:

Declarer now has to lose a trick in the suit, however he plays. In particular, if he leads the jack on the next round you will cover in order to promote partner's ten. A sound guideline is available to help you here: **do not cover the first of touching honors**. Allow the queen to pass and then cover the jack.

Here is a similar situation:

♠ J 10 5
♠ Q 9 4   ♠ K 8 3
♠ A 7 6 2

Declarer leads the jack from dummy. If you make the mistake of covering the first of touching honors he will win with the ace and lead back towards the ten, scoring three spade tricks. Allow the jack to pass to partner's queen and declarer will make only two spade tricks. If he leads the ten on the second round, you will cover to promote partner's nine.

Let's look at one of these situations when the honor is led from the closed hand instead of from dummy:

```
              ♠ A 7 3
            ┌─────────┐
  ♠ K 5 4   │         │   ♠ 10 8 6
            └─────────┘
              ♠ Q J 9 2
```

This situation is just the same, of course. If you cover the queen (the first of touching honors) declarer will score four tricks in the suit. From West's point of view this is more difficult to visualize than when the Q-J-9-x combination is visible in the dummy. Nevertheless, the appearance of the queen from the South hand strongly suggests that declarer holds the jack too. It is sound defense for you to play low, retaining the king.

Remember the point we noted earlier. Declarer will rarely lead an honor from his hand unless he can afford it to be covered.

Covering may crash an honor in partner's hand

One of the most horrible accidents that can happen to defenders is that they 'crash honors'. In other words, one of them chooses to play an honor to a trick only to find that their partner is forced to play an honor too. Suppose declarer is in 6♠ with this trump holding:

```
              ♠ Q 8 7 4 2
            ┌─────────┐
  ♠ A       │         │   ♠ K 9
            └─────────┘
              ♠ J 10 6 5 3
```

He wins the opening lead in dummy and plays the queen of trumps. If you cover with the king, declarer will tell the story for months!

How can you tell that it is wrong to cover? Remember that the purpose of covering is to promote lesser cards. This is not possible here (except in the very unlikely case where declarer has A-10-x-x), so you should play the nine.

Playing low may gain in a different way. Perhaps the trump suit actually lies like this:

```
              ♠ Q 8 7 4 2
            ┌─────────┐
  ♠ 5       │         │   ♠ K 9
            └─────────┘
              ♠ A J 10 6 3
```

When dummy's queen is not covered, declarer may place West with the king and rise with the ace, in the hope that the king is singleton. Declarer may also hold A-J-10 sixth, in which case he is almost certain to play for the drop.

Summary

✓ Cover an honor only when there is a prospect of promoting a lesser card, either in your own hand or in partner's.

✓ Beware of covering with a queen when this may save declarer a guess. If he has led an honor from his hand, he can usually afford to have you cover the card and may actually welcome it.

✓ Do not cover the first of touching honors. When an honor is led from the closed hand (for example the queen when the ace is in dummy), it is likely that it is one of touching honors.

✓ When declarer has long trumps in both hands beware of covering when this may crash an honor in partner's hand.

COVER AN HONOR WITH AN HONOR

1)

♠ Q 10 8 7

♠ K 2

After bidding of 1♠ - 4♠, South wins the opening lead in dummy and plays the ♠Q. Do you cover or not? What is the reason for your decision?

2)

♦ A 7 5

♦ K 8 3

♦ Q led

South is in 3NT and leads the queen from his hand on the first round of diamonds. Do you cover or not? What is the reason for your decision?

3)

♣ A Q 9 3

♣ K 10 2

♣ J led

After bidding of 1NT - 3NT South leads the club jack on the first round of the suit. Do you cover or not? What is the reason for your decision?

4)

♠ K Q 10 5 2
♥ J 4
♦ A K J
♣ K Q 6

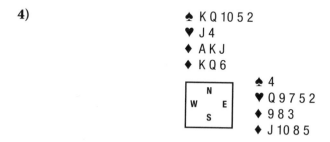

♠ 4
♥ Q 9 7 5 2
♦ 9 8 3
♣ J 10 8 5

When South opened 1♠, North bid Blackwood, heard about two aces, and bid 6♠. Declarer wins the trump lead in the dummy and calls for the ♥J. Do you cover? What is the reason for your choice?

ANSWERS

1) You **should not** cover the ♠Q. Covering would promote a trick only if declarer held A-x-x-x-x. In that case he is more likely to have played the ace on the first round. A cover can lose in two ways. Firstly, your partner could hold a singleton ace. Secondly, declarer might hold six or seven trumps headed by the ace-jack. If you produce a smooth low card in that case he may attempt to drop a singleton king from your partner's hand.

2) You **should not** cover the ♦Q. Declarer surely holds the ♦J backing the queen and you should not cover the first of touching honors in case this sets up a finesse on the second round. If declarer holds Q-J-9-x, a cover will let him score four tricks from the suit.

3) You **should** cover the ♣J. By doing so, you hope to promote partner's 8-x-x-x, should declarer have started with only a doubleton in the suit. If you play low, it is easy to see what will happen. The jack will win the first round and a subsequent finesse will give declarer four tricks in the suit.

4) You **should not** cover the ♥J. Declarer's Blackwood response reveals that your partner holds an ace. If this is the ace of hearts, declarer's heart holding may be headed by the K-10. In that case he must guess the hearts correctly to make the contract! If you cover the heart jack with the queen you will save him a guess. Play low smoothly and he may think that you cannot hold the queen. He will rise with the king, playing you for the ace instead, and then lose two heart tricks. (If your partner holds the club ace instead, it can hardly matter whether you cover the ♥J.)

C H A P T E R

SECOND HAND LOW

 If you do not play the ace second-in-hand, the declarer may win the trick and discard his worthless cards in the suit. *J.B. Elwell*

In Chapter 14 we looked at the defender's guideline 'third hand high' and saw that there were many occasions when it should not be applied. The time has now come to look at the defender's play in the second seat. Here the general advice is: **play low in second seat**. This guideline applies whether or not your high card will win the trick. Here your high card is an ace:

The ♠4 appears from the closed hand. If you leap in with the ace declarer will score two tricks from the suit. Aces are designed to capture kings and queens. Playing them on thin air will often cost a trick.

In the next position your high card would not win the trick:

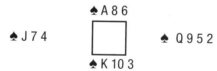

You are sitting West and declarer leads the ♠3. If you contribute the four, following the guideline, declarer will score only two tricks in the suit. If instead you mistakenly play the jack, declarer can win with the ace and finesse the ten on the way back, scoring an undeserved three spade tricks.

Another reason to play low in second seat is that you may give declarer a guess. Suppose declarer is in a slam and has to play this side suit:

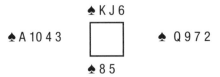

All the other suits are solid, we will say, and he has to guess correctly in spades to make the slam. With bated breath he leads the ♠5. Not very difficult for him if you rise with the ace, is it?

Splitting honors to prevent a finesse

When you are second to play and hold two cards of equal rank, usually honors, you may need to play high in order to stop declarer from taking a winning finesse.

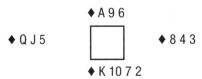

Declarer leads the ♦2 and you must choose a card in the West seat. If you play low, declarer is likely to insert the nine. Once he has recovered from his surprise at the nine winning the trick, he will score three further tricks in the suit. To prevent such a finesse you must 'split your honors'. You must insert the queen or jack to force dummy's ace and you will then be assured of a trick in the suit.

Second hand high to avoid an endplay

Suppose declarer is playing in a suit contract such as 4♠ and you hold a double-ton honor in one of the side suits. Playing second-hand-low from such a holding may result in you being endplayed. Look at this deal:

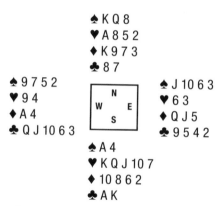

                    ♠ K Q 8
                    ♥ A 8 5 2
                    ♦ K 9 7 3
                    ♣ 8 7

    ♠ 9 7 5 2   ♠ J 10 6 3
    ♥ 9 4   N   ♥ 6 3
    ♦ A 4   W   E   ♦ Q J 5
    ♣ Q J 10 6 3   S   ♣ 9 5 4 2

                    ♠ A 4
                    ♥ K Q J 10 7
                    ♦ 10 8 6 2
                    ♣ A K

You lead the ♣Q against 6♥ and South wins with the ace. Suppose he plays the ♦2 at Trick 2. If you play low, he will make the contract. He will win with dummy's king, draw trumps and eliminate the black suits, throwing a diamond from his hand. When he leads another diamond you will have to win with the bare ace and give him a ruff-and-sluff. Away will go declarer's last diamond and he will have twelve tricks. If instead you rise with the ace on the first round, declarer cannot avoid a second diamond loser.

It is similarly dangerous to play low from a doubleton ace in the trump suit. Again declarer may be able to eliminate one or more side suits before throwing you in with the bare ace. That's what might happen here:

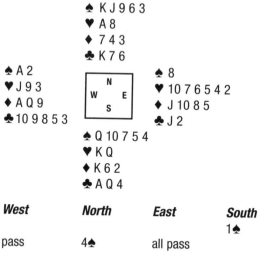

                    ♠ K J 9 6 3
                    ♥ A 8
                    ♦ 7 4 3
                    ♣ K 7 6

    ♠ A 2   ♠ 8
    ♥ J 9 3   N   ♥ 10 7 6 5 4 2
    ♦ A Q 9   W   E   ♦ J 10 8 5
    ♣ 10 9 8 5 3   S   ♣ J 2

                    ♠ Q 10 7 5 4
                    ♥ K Q
                    ♦ K 6 2
                    ♣ A Q 4

West	North	East	South
			1♠
pass	4♠	all pass	

Declarer wins your ♣10 lead with the ace and plays the four of trumps. What is your reaction?

Some defenders would play low, with impressive smoothness. 'I thought declarer might have a guess in the trump suit,' they will explain afterwards. The effect will be costly. After winning the first round of trumps, declarer will play his winners in hearts and clubs. He will then exit with a trump to the bare ace, leaving West end-played. If he plays a diamond, declarer will score a trick with the king. If instead he plays a club or a heart, this will concede a ruff-and-sluff.

Suppose, on this deal, that West does defend well by rising with the ace of trumps on the first round. Will the contract then go down? Declarer will win West's exit, draw the outstanding trumps and eliminate clubs and hearts. He will then lead a low diamond from dummy. If East follows with the eight or the five, West will have to overtake with the nine and will again be endplayed. To prevent this from happening, East must rise with the jack or ten. Declarer cannot then avoid the loss of three diamond tricks and the contract will fail.

If West rises with the ace of trumps on the first round of the suit, he avoids the endplay. He can exit safely in any suit except diamonds and declarer will have to play the diamond suit himself. How likely was it that declarer was missing the queen of trumps and had a potential guess in the spade suit? It was very unlikely. He held at least five of the missing six spades and was therefore a huge favorite to hold the queen.

Second hand high to break declarer's communications

When there is a long suit in an otherwise entryless dummy, you can often gain by inserting an honor in second position. Take the West cards here:

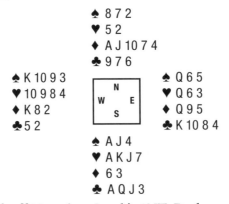

```
            ♠ 8 7 2
            ♥ 5 2
            ♦ A J 10 7 4
            ♣ 9 7 6
♠ K 10 9 3              ♠ Q 6 5
♥ 10 9 8 4    N        ♥ Q 6 3
♦ K 8 2     W   E      ♦ Q 9 5
♣ 5 2         S        ♣ K 10 8 4
            ♠ A J 4
            ♥ A K J 7
            ♦ 6 3
            ♣ A Q J 3
```

You lead the ♥10 against South's 3NT. Declarer wins partner's queen with the ace and leads a diamond. How do you read the situation?

If you follow with a spot-card, declarer will play the jack from dummy. Your partner now has two choices. If he wins the queen, declarer can finesse the ♦10 on the next round and score four diamond tricks. East does better to duck, but it will not beat the contract. Declarer will use the extra entry to finesse the ♣Q successfully. He can then return to dummy with the ♦A and finesse the ♣J. That will give him nine tricks.

See how much better the defense goes if you rise with the ♦K on the first round! If declarer wins with the ace, he will make only one diamond trick. If he ducks, and finesses you for the queen on the next round, he will make no diamond tricks at all. Either way, he will go down.

Second hand high to prevent a ruffing finesse

Take the West cards here, on a deal where many defenders would go wrong:

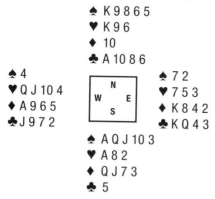

  South arrives in 6♠ and wins your ♥Q with the ace. He draws trumps in two rounds and leads the ♦3 from his hand. What will you do?

  Suppose you are unwilling to expend your precious ace on a mere ten-spot. Partner will win with the king and set up your heart trick. Much good will it do you! Declarer will subsequently lead the ♦Q from his hand, taking a ruffing finesse against your ace. Whether or not you cover, the diamond suit will provide him with a discard for dummy's heart loser. The slam will be made.

  You should play your ace on the first round. With partner's king of diamonds sitting over the dummy, no subsequent ruffing finesse will be possible and the slam will go one down.

Second hand high to preserve partner's entry

When declarer needs to knock out two stoppers in his main suit, it is often important that the defenders take their stoppers in the right order. This may involve playing 'second hand high'. Take the East cards here:

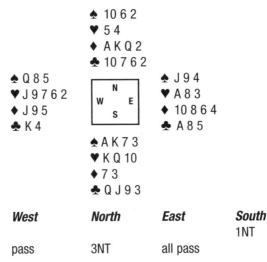

	♠ 10 6 2		
	♥ 5 4		
	♦ A K Q 2		
	♣ 10 7 6 2		

West	North	East	South
			1NT
pass	3NT	all pass	

Your partner leads the ♥6 and you win with the ace, returning the ♥8. Declarer wins with the queen, crosses to dummy with a diamond and leads a low club. Can you see what is happening?

Since ducking a spade would bring his total to only eight tricks even if the suit did break 3-3, declarer is forced to play on clubs. To beat the contract you must play 'second hand high', rising with the ace of clubs. You can then set up partner's hearts while he still has the ♣K as an entry.

Suppose instead you play low on the first round of clubs. If partner wins with the king and clears the heart suit, declarer can safely knock out the other club. You will have no heart to return. If instead partner allows the queen of clubs to win, declarer cannot go wrong. Whether he perseveres with clubs or gives up a spade, he will arrive at nine tricks.

Perhaps you are worried that the clubs lie like this:

It is still right to rise with the ace and clear the hearts. It's true that declarer should continue with king and another club, since he cannot allow West to gain the lead. There are plenty of less-than-perfect declarers, though, who will return to dummy and finesse into the doubleton queen. In any case, if you play low on the first club, the contract will be easily made.

Second hand high to set up a winner

Even in a trump contract you may need to take your stoppers in the right order. Here the setting trick can be set up only from the West seat:

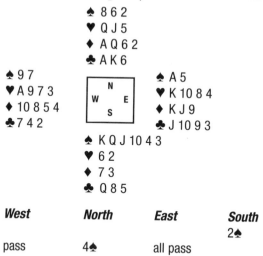

```
                    ♠ 8 6 2
                    ♥ Q J 5
                    ♦ A Q 6 2
                    ♣ A K 6
   ♠ 9 7                            ♠ A 5
   ♥ A 9 7 3          N             ♥ K 10 8 4
   ♦ 10 8 5 4      W     E          ♦ K J 9
   ♣ 7 4 2            S             ♣ J 10 9 3
                    ♠ K Q J 10 4 3
                    ♥ 6 2
                    ♦ 7 3
                    ♣ Q 8 5
```

West	North	East	South
			2♠
pass	4♠	all pass	

South's weak 2♠ is raised to 4♠ and you lead a trump to partner's ace. Declarer wins the ♣J return with dummy's ace, draws a second round of trumps and leads a low heart from his hand. What will you do?

Your partner's ♣J denied the queen, so you can place declarer with five trump tricks, at least three club tricks and the ♦A. A heart trick will bring his total to ten, so you must act quickly to set up a fourth trick for the defense. Rise with the ♥A and switch to a diamond. Declarer has little option but to finesse. When your partner wins with the ♦K he will cash a heart for one down. If instead you play low on the first heart, your partner will have to win the trick. He cannot attack diamonds from his side of the table and there will be no way to beat the contract.

Summary

✓ Generally play low in the second seat unless you can see a clear purpose in a higher card.

✓ Reasons for playing high include: you wish to clear partner's suit, or to establish the setting trick, before partner's entry is removed; you need to disrupt declarer's communications when he has a long suit in an entryless dummy; you do not wish to set up a ruffing finesse.

✓ When defending a suit contract, be wary of playing low from a doubleton honor. You may be endplayed with the honor later.

SECOND HAND LOW

NOW TRY THESE...

1)

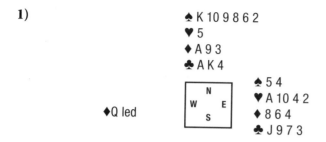

♠Q led

♠ K 10 9 8 6 2
♥ 5
♦ A 9 3
♣ A K 4

♠ 5 4
♥ A 10 4 2
♦ 8 6 4
♣ J 9 7 3

South, who opened 1♠, is now playing in 6♠. He wins the opening lead with dummy's ♦A and leads the ♥5. Do you play the ace or not? What is the reason for your decision?

2)

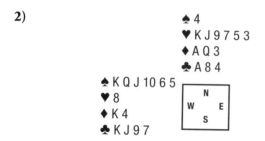

♠ 4
♥ K J 9 7 5 3
♦ A Q 3
♣ A 8 4

♠ K Q J 10 6 5
♥ 8
♦ K 4
♣ K J 9 7

South, who opened 1♥, is now playing in 6♥ despite your 1♠ overcall. He wins the opening ♠K lead with his ace and leads the ♦6. Do you play the king or not? What is the reason for your decision?

ANSWERS

1) You should not play the ace or even think of doing so. There are two reasons why. If declarer's hearts are headed by the K-J, you will save him a guess by rising with the ace. He will be able to discard a diamond loser on the ♥K and surely make the contract. Play low smoothly and he may finesse the jack, losing to your partner's queen. Another possibility is that declarer's hearts are headed by the Q-J. If you rise with the ace you will set up a ruffing finesse against partner's king, again permitting a diamond discard from dummy. Remember this general rule: when a singleton is led from dummy do not play an ace unless you can see where the setting tricks are coming from.

2) You should rise with the king of diamonds, wary of playing low and leaving yourself with a bare honor when declarer has plenty of trumps in both hands. Suppose this is the full deal:

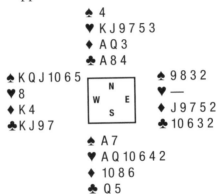

```
              ♠ 4
              ♥ K J 9 7 5 3
              ♦ A Q 3
              ♣ A 8 4
 ♠ K Q J 10 6 5              ♠ 9 8 3 2
 ♥ 8            N            ♥ —
 ♦ K 4      W     E          ♦ J 9 7 5 2
 ♣ K J 9 7      S            ♣ 10 6 3 2
              ♠ A 7
              ♥ A Q 10 6 4 2
              ♦ 10 8 6
              ♣ Q 5
```

If you play low on the first round of diamonds, declarer will finesse the queen, draw trumps and ruff his spade loser. When he subsequently leads a second round of diamonds from his hand, he can allow your king to win. You will then have to lead a club from the king or concede a ruff-and-sluff. Play the king on the first round and you are safe. Don't worry that declarer may have started with ♦ J-x-x. If that's the case, there is nothing you can do.

C H A P T E R **18**

CAPTURE AN HONOR
WITH AN HONOR

 When some well-planned ruse has found the opposition thrown
into confusion by the clever capture of a trick or two which they
never had dreamed it possible to lose, you may feel the elation that
is part of bridge when the game is played to the full measure of its
theory *J.B. Elwell*

What is the main purpose of aces? To capture kings and queens! That's true as
far as it goes. It's certainly not very attractive to lead an ace and collect two
minnow-cards from the opponents. Nor is it normally wise to rise with an ace
in second position. Let's see what lies behind the guideline that you should
always capture an honor with an honor:

Declarer leads a low heart to dummy's king. Happy to capture a big card,
you win with the ace. The effect of this is that your partner's jack will now also
win a trick. If instead you allow dummy's ♥K to win, declarer will lead a second
round of hearts from dummy and you will waste your ace on a lowly two-spot.
Once declarer has stopped laughing he will bring in the suit for just one loser.

Does that mean you should always capture an honor when you can? No, indeed. There are several situations in which you might choose to hold up. Let's see some of them.

Not capturing gives declarer a guess

Sometimes winning one of declarer's honors immediately will force him to make the right play on the next round. Suppose you are East here:

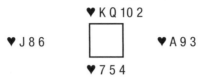

♥ K Q 10 2

♥ J 8 6   ♥ A 9 3

♥ 7 5 4

Declarer leads a low heart to the king. If you win with the ace he will finesse the ten on the next round and score three heart tricks. Instead you should follow smoothly with a low card, pretending that you don't hold the ace. Declarer will return to his hand in some other suit and lead another heart towards dummy. He will then have a guess to make. If your partner started with A-8-6, he should play the queen from dummy. As the cards actually lie, the winning play is to finesse the ten. Put declarer to such guesses as often as you can! A pile of extra tricks will come your way.

Not capturing makes declarer waste an entry

Sometimes declarer has few entries to dummy and a choice of finesses to take. By letting him think that one of his finesses has succeeded and can be repeated, you may cause him to misuse his entries. Look at this deal:

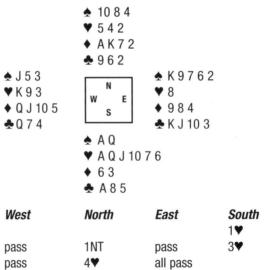

♠ 10 8 4
♥ 5 4 2
♦ A K 7 2
♣ 9 6 2

♠ J 5 3
♥ K 9 3
♦ Q J 10 5
♣ Q 7 4

♠ K 9 7 6 2
♥ 8
♦ 9 8 4
♣ K J 10 3

♠ A Q
♥ A Q J 10 7 6
♦ 6 3
♣ A 8 5

West	North	East	South
			1♥
pass	1NT	pass	3♥
pass	4♥	all pass	

Sitting West, you lead the ♦Q against game in hearts. Declarer wins in the dummy and plays a trump to the queen and your king. What now?

The answer is that declarer will make the contract! Knowing that he must avoid a spade loser, he will take the spade finesse when he is in dummy for the last time. Suppose instead that you are quick-witted enough to duck smoothly when the ♥Q is finessed. There is a good chance that declarer will return to dummy in diamonds and repeat the heart finesse. It will be a very enjoyable moment for you when East shows out. Declarer will eventually have to lead spades from his own hand, losing a trick in the suit and going one down.

Not capturing kills an entry to dummy

Even when the lie of the suit is perfectly obvious to declarer, it can be right to refuse to capture an honor. Your purpose is to kill declarer's communications. Take the East cards on this deal:

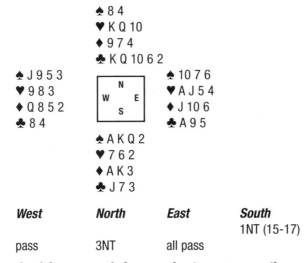

	♠ 8 4		
	♥ K Q 10		
	♦ 9 7 4		
	♣ K Q 10 6 2		

West	North	East	South
			1NT (15-17)
pass	3NT	all pass	

Unwilling to lead from a weak four-card suit, partner strikes out with the ♥9 (top of nothing). Declarer plays dummy's king and you must decide what to do. Can you see why it would be costly to win?

Let's see what happens if you do win. You cannot safely continue hearts and will have to switch to spades or diamonds. Declarer will win the trick and play on clubs, knocking out your ace. It does you no good to hold up the ♣A until the third round because declarer has an entry to dummy in hearts. He will make at least ten tricks, whatever you play next.

Look back to the diagram and see the effect of holding up your ♥A at Trick 1. Your A-J will then be poised over dummy's Q-10, preventing declarer from crossing to dummy in the suit. When he plays on clubs your partner will play high-low to show a doubleton. You will then hold up the ♣A until the third round (refusing to capture an honor with an honor in two different suits!). Twist and turn as he may, declarer goes one down.

Holding up a king may be similarly effective. Take the East cards here:

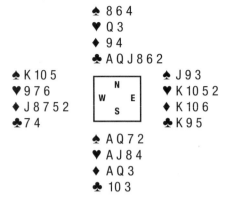

After an auction of 1NT – 3NT your partner leads the ♦5 to your king and South's ace. Declarer now runs the ♣10. What should you do?

Suppose you are in a hurry to return partner's suit and you win your ♣K at the first opportunity. You won't enjoy what happens next. Declarer will face his cards, claiming the contract!

It would be a bad mistake to win the first round of clubs. It is obvious that declarer has a second diamond stopper or he would have held up the ace. If you let the ♣10 win the trick, what will declarer do next? He will probably play a club to the queen! Now is the time to win the king. Declarer will make only one club trick and go several down.

Not capturing avoids an endplay

Suppose declarer draws trumps, eliminates two of the side suits and then plays on the remaining suit. A situation may arise where you will be endplayed if you win the first round of this final side suit. Let's look straight away at a full-deal example of this:

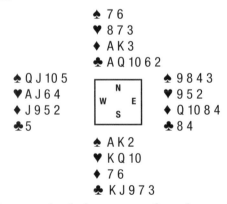

Sitting West, you lead the queen of spades against South's small slam in clubs. Declarer wins with the ace, draws trumps in two rounds and eliminates both spades and diamonds (by cashing the winners and ruffing the third round). The lead is in dummy and these cards remain:

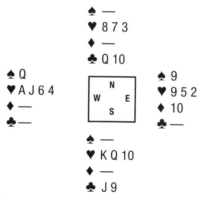

♠ —
♥ 8 7 3
♦ —
♣ Q 10

♠ Q
♥ A J 6 4
♦ —
♣ —

♠ 9
♥ 9 5 2
♦ 10
♣ —

♠ —
♥ K Q 10
♦ —
♣ J 9

How should you react when declarer leads a heart to the king? If you 'do what comes naturally' and win with the ace, you will regret it. A heart return will be into declarer's Q-10 tenace. If you play the ♠Q instead, this will give a ruff-and-discard. To beat the contract you must allow South's ♥K to win the trick. He will then return to dummy with a trump to lead a second round of hearts towards his hand. When a low card appears from East and declarer starts to ponder his play, you can put him out of his misery and claim one down.

How do you know that it is right to hold up the ace? You must count declarer's hand. He has shown up with five clubs, three spades and two diamonds. That is ten cards out of thirteen, so he must have three hearts. In that case you can guarantee beating the contract by holding up the ace of hearts. Suppose instead that declarer had started with Q-10-5 of diamonds instead of 10-5. When he subsequently played a heart to the king, you would know that he had started with only two hearts. In that case you would win the king of hearts with the ace, hoping that your partner held the heart queen.

The deal illustrates that you cannot afford to take a brief snooze when declarer is playing on suits in which you have no interest. To defend well, it is essential to 'count the hand' — in other words, to determine the shape of declarer's hand. Players who are unwilling to do this often find that they have to guess in crucial situations. And you know what that means. Some of the time they will guess wrong.

Summary

✓ Winning one honor with another is usually beneficial. You are likely to promote the value of lesser cards held by your side.

✓ The most common reason for refusing to win with an honor is that you are holding up an ace to kill declarer's communications.

✓ Another reason to hold up is to give declarer a guess in a finessing situation. If declarer plays towards K-Q-10, rising with the king, you can play low smoothly in fourth position, keeping the position of the ace a secret.

CAPTURE AN HONOR WITH AN HONOR

1)

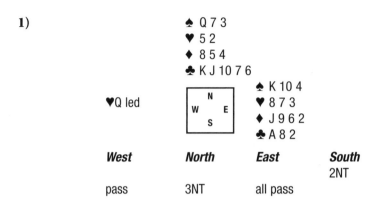

♥Q led

	♠ Q 7 3	
	♥ 5 2	
	♦ 8 5 4	
	♣ K J 10 7 6	

East:
♠ K 10 4
♥ 8 7 3
♦ J 9 6 2
♣ A 8 2

West	North	East	South
			2NT
pass	3NT	all pass	

Your partner leads the ♥Q against 3NT and declarer wins with the ace. South now leads the ♣4, your partner playing the five and dummy the jack. Will you hold up or not? What is the reason for your choice?

Suppose you do hold up and declarer returns to his hand with the ♦A, leading a second club to the ten. How will you know what to do then?

2)

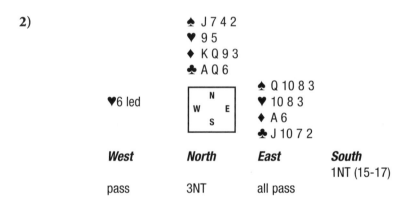

♥6 led

	♠ J 7 4 2	
	♥ 9 5	
	♦ K Q 9 3	
	♣ A Q 6	

East:
♠ Q 10 8 3
♥ 10 8 3
♦ A 6
♣ J 10 7 2

West	North	East	South
			1NT (15-17)
pass	3NT	all pass	

Partner's ♥6 lead is covered by the five, eight and jack. Declarer now plays a diamond to West's two and dummy's king. Do you win with the ace or not? What is the reason for your decision?

ANSWERS

1) You should hold up the ♣A, aiming to cut communications between declarer's hand and the dummy. This may be the whole deal:

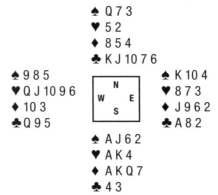

```
                    ♠ Q 7 3
                    ♥ 5 2
                    ♦ 8 5 4
                    ♣ K J 10 7 6
   ♠ 9 8 5                          ♠ K 10 4
   ♥ Q J 10 9 6      N              ♥ 8 7 3
   ♦ 10 3         W     E           ♦ J 9 6 2
   ♣ Q 9 5           S              ♣ A 8 2
                    ♠ A J 6 2
                    ♥ A K 4
                    ♦ A K Q 7
                    ♣ 4 3
```

Declarer wins the ♥Q lead with the ace and plays the four of clubs to the five and jack, which you should duck since dummy has no side entries. He returns to his hand with the ♦A and plays a second club to the ten. How will you know whether to hold up again? Your partner's second card in clubs will tell you! The five followed by the nine (a count signal) shows an odd number of clubs. Declarer therefore started with only two and you must take your ace on the second round. If you fail to do so, declarer will gratefully pocket his second club trick and take the spade finesse to bring his total to nine tricks.

If declarer had started with ♣Q-9-4, your partner's second club would have been the three (his high-low signal of the five followed by the three would then show an even number). You would then hold up the ace of clubs for a second time. This would beat the contract if South did not hold the ♠J.

2) You should not win with the ace, nor give any sign that you hold this card. A likely lie of the diamond suit is this:

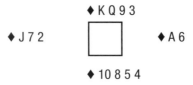

```
              ♦ K Q 9 3
   ♦ J 7 2                  ♦ A 6
              ♦ 10 8 5 4
```

If you duck smoothly when declarer plays a diamond to the king, you give him a guess in the suit. He may return to his hand and play a second diamond to the queen. Now you can win with the ace and clear partner's heart suit. His ♦J will serve as an entry to the established heart winners

CHAPTER 19

LEAD THROUGH STRENGTH

 The fundamental idea of leading through strength is to help your partner make his high cards by allowing him to play after the exposed hand. *J.B. Elwell*

What do you make of the defensive guideline: **lead through strength and up to weakness**? I don't rate it as very helpful myself. When you are defending you have so many different things to think about. To decide on the best switch or continuation may require considerable thought. Anyone who resorts solely to generalizations such as this will never make a good defender.

We can see the basis for the rule by looking at this single-suit position:

```
              ♠ 8 6 3
♠ K J 9 2     [    ]     ♠ 7 5 4
              ♠ A Q 10
```

If East is on play, leading a spade 'up to the weakness in dummy' will work fine. If instead it were West's lead then he would do well to play some other suit, rather than leading away from his honors into strength.

It will not surprise you to hear that there are several exceptions to this rather simplistic guideline. Let's see some of them.

Leading up to weakness would do declarer's work for him

When calculating if a particular switch is safe, or desirable, you must not only consider declarer's two holdings but also your own. Leading from an honor up to weakness in the dummy may not be at all safe. You may be allowing declarer to take a finesse that he could not take on his own. Suppose you are East here:

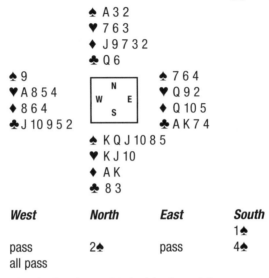

West	North	East	South
			1♠
pass	2♠	pass	4♠
all pass			

Your partner leads the ♣J and it holds the trick. Partner's ♣5 continuation is covered by the queen and king, declarer following, and you must calculate the best return.

Let's look at each suit in turn. In clubs, partner led the ♣5 (his fourth-best card) on the second round. The ♣2 has not yet appeared and the most likely situation is that West started with five clubs and a third round of the suit would give declarer a ruff-and-discard. A diamond return is risky, since declarer might hold A-K-x. Perhaps you think that a heart switch, up to dummy's weakness, looks safe. It is not! If declarer's hearts are headed by the A-J-10 or K-J-10, a heart switch will allow him to take two finesses in the suit. Left to his own devices, he has only one entry to dummy (the ♠A) and will be able to finesse only once in the suit. That leaves us with a spade switch. Yes, that's the best idea. Only if declarer has precisely K-J-10-x-x will this switch save him a guess.

When you switch to spades, the contract is doomed. Declarer cannot avoid two heart losers to go with his two club losers.

Leading up to strength cuts declarer's communications

Suppose declarer is playing in a high spade contract and has this impressive diamond side suit:

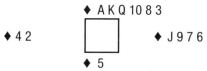

```
                     ♦ A K Q 10 8 3
   ♦ 4 2                                 ♦ J 9 7 6
                     ♦ 5
```

Before he can take two discards on the suit, he will have to draw trumps. If the defenders can play a round of diamonds early on, they may break declarer's communications and prevent at least one of the discards. Here is a complete deal that illustrates this theme. You have the East cards:

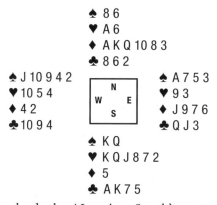

```
                  ♠ 8 6
                  ♥ A 6
                  ♦ A K Q 10 8 3
                  ♣ 8 6 2
  ♠ J 10 9 4 2            N        ♠ A 7 5 3
  ♥ 10 5 4          W         E    ♥ 9 3
  ♦ 4 2                   S        ♦ J 9 7 6
  ♣ 10 9 4                         ♣ Q J 3
                  ♠ K Q
                  ♥ K Q J 8 7 2
                  ♦ 5
                  ♣ A K 7 5
```

Your partner leads the ♠J against South's contract of 6♥. You win with the ace, the queen falling from declarer. What now?

Many defenders would switch to a club. There's not much point in it, is there? South surely holds the ♣A. He will simply win the club switch, draw trumps and play dummy's top diamonds, discarding his two club losers.

Now try something more dynamic. Switch to a diamond, into dummy's strength! Since declarer has only a singleton diamond, this breaks his link with the dummy. He will not be a happy man. The best he can do is to draw two rounds of trumps, with the king and ace, followed by two more rounds of diamonds. All would be well if the diamonds broke 3-3 or the defender with the doubleton diamond did not hold the last trump. As the cards lie, your defense will succeed. West will ruff the third diamond, as declarer throws his last club loser, and the slam will go down.

Declarer has threatening diamonds on the next deal too, but the potential entry to them lies in a different suit:

```
                        ♠ 6 5
                        ♥ K Q 5
                        ♦ K Q J 6
                        ♣ 8 7 5 3
        ♠ J 9 2                         ♠ 7
        ♥ 9 8 3            N            ♥ A J 10 4
        ♦ 10 8 7 4     W       E        ♦ A 9 2
        ♣ 10 9 2          S            ♣ A Q J 6 4
                        ♠ A K Q 10 8 4 3
                        ♥ 7 6 2
                        ♦ 5 3
                        ♣ K
```

West	North	East	South
		1♣	1♠
pass	2♦	pass	4♠
all pass			

You are sitting East and your partner leads the ♣10 to your ace, the king appearing from declarer. How will you continue the defense?

Most of the world's defenders would play another club, leading up to the weakness in dummy. This will give declarer an easy ride. He will ruff, draw trumps and play on diamonds. Holding up the ace for one round will not help you very much because declarer can force an entry to dummy in hearts. One of his heart losers will go away on the third diamond honor and that will be ten tricks.

BY THE WAY

It was not particularly difficult to see the potential of a heart switch on this deal, when your hearts were as strong as A-J-10-x. The same defense would have been necessary when your hearts were weaker, such as A-10-9-x or A-J-8-x. You would have to hope that partner had some help for you in the heart suit.

How can you prevent this? You must attack the side entry to dummy's diamond suit by switching to the ♥J at Trick 2! Declarer has no counter to this. He has to win the heart trick or you will simply cash two more aces to beat the contract. Suppose he draws trumps next and plays a diamond to the king. Your partner will play the ♦8 — a high spot card to indicate an even number of diamonds. Expecting declarer to hold two diamonds, you will now hold up the diamond ace. When a second diamond is played, you will win with the ace and exit safely in clubs. Declarer cannot then avoid the loss of two hearts and the two minor-suit aces.

Leading up to strength sets up a winner

Another good reason for leading up to apparent strength, rather than exiting passively, is that you need to set up an extra winner or two in order to beat the contract. There is no real excuse for misdefending on the next deal but many East players would do so. You are not among them, I realize. But, well… why not take the East cards and find out?

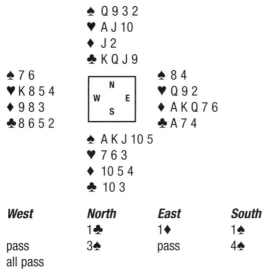

	♠ Q 9 3 2	
	♥ A J 10	
	♦ J 2	
	♣ K Q J 9	

♠ 7 6
♥ K 8 5 4
♦ 9 8 3
♣ 8 6 5 2

♠ 8 4
♥ Q 9 2
♦ A K Q 7 6
♣ A 7 4

♠ A K J 10 5
♥ 7 6 3
♦ 10 5 4
♣ 10 3

West	North	East	South
	1♣	1♦	1♠
pass	3♠	pass	4♠
all pass			

North overbids and South arrives in a poor spade game. Your partner leads the ♦3 and you win with the queen. When you cash a second diamond winner, partner plays the eight and now you know that he started with three diamonds. What next?

Suppose you exit passively, switching to a trump. It is not difficult to foresee what will happen. Declarer will draw trumps and set up the clubs. He can then discard his two heart losers on the surplus club winners and ruff a diamond for his tenth trick.

How should you defend? You can see three obvious winners for the defense — two diamonds and a club. To beat the contract you will need one more trick, either from the trump suit or from hearts. If partner has a winner in the trump suit it cannot run away, so you must address the situation where partner has the king of hearts. At Trick 3 you must steel yourself to lead into dummy's heart strength. Your bravery is rewarded when West produces the king, forcing dummy's ace. It is time for declarer to give a helpless shrug of the shoulders (and perhaps prepare his complaint about partner's overbidding). When you win with the ace of clubs, you will cash the setting trick in hearts.

Summary

✓ 'Lead through strength and up to weakness' has some value as a guideline for beginners. Defense usually requires thought and effort, however. You must decide whether you need to be aggressive — to take or set up tricks before declarer can establish discards — or whether you should defend passively. This sort of decision requires several factors to be taken into account. Seven-word mantras are of limited use!

✓ Leading up to weakness in the dummy is not necessarily safe if you are leading from an honor. You may allow declarer to take a finesse that he could not otherwise have taken.

✓ When declarer has a suit in dummy headed by top cards, you can sometimes break his communications by playing on that suit.

LEAD THROUGH STRENGTH

1)

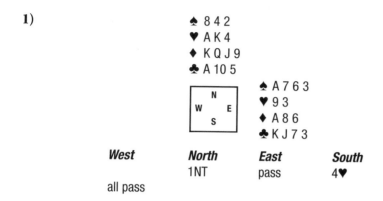

♠ 8 4 2
♥ A K 4
♦ K Q J 9
♣ A 10 5

♠ A 7 6 3
♥ 9 3
♦ A 8 6
♣ K J 7 3

West	North	East	South
	1NT	pass	4♥
all pass			

Your partner leads the ♠Q and you win with the ace, the king falling from South. What will you do next? How can this contract be beaten?

2)

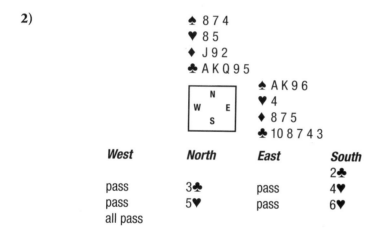

♠ 8 7 4
♥ 8 5
♦ J 9 2
♣ A K Q 9 5

♠ A K 9 6
♥ 4
♦ 8 7 5
♣ 10 8 7 4 3

West	North	East	South
			2♣
pass	3♣	pass	4♥
pass	5♥	pass	6♥
all pass			

Partner answers your prayers by leading a spade. You win his ♠3 lead with the king and declarer follows with the ♠J. What next?

ANSWERS

1) Many defenders would continue with another spade but it is easy to see what will happen. After ruffing the second spade, declarer will draw trumps and set up the diamonds. He will then score at least six hearts, three diamonds and the ♣A. At Trick 3 you should switch to a low club, hoping to find partner with ♣Q. You will beat the contract if the cards lie like this:

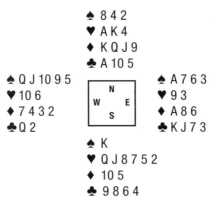

Declarer will hold up the ♣A for one round, hoping that the defender with the ♦A has only two clubs. Not today!

2) It is almost impossible that a second spade will stand up after South's advance to 6♥. You should switch to a club, up to dummy's strength. This will work spectacularly well if partner is void in clubs and can ruff. When partner has two clubs, you may cut declarer off from the dummy:

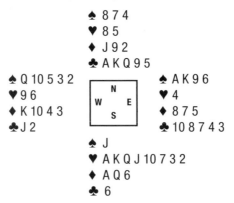

Declarer can throw one diamond on the second club winner. Whether he tries another club next or the diamond finesse, he will go one down.

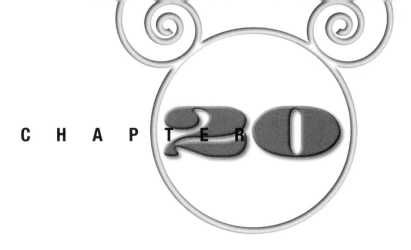

C H A P T E R **30**

DISCARD FROM YOUR WEAKEST SUIT

 To those who have not taken the time to analyze hands thoroughly, the discard of a card which may possibly make, naturally seems the waste of a trick. **J.B. Elwell**

When you first play the game, discarding can be difficult. A simple guideline is: discard from your weakest suit. Take the East cards on this slam deal:

```
              ♠ 7 6 4
              ♥ A Q 3
              ♦ A K 4
              ♣ K Q 7 2
♠ K Q J 9 3        ┌─────────┐        ♠ 8 2
♥ 8 5             │    N    │        ♥ J 10 4 2
♦ 9 8 6           │  W   E  │        ♦ 10 7 5 3
♣ 10 5 3          │    S    │        ♣ 9 8 4
                  └─────────┘
              ♠ A 10 5
              ♥ K 9 7 6
              ♦ Q J 2
              ♣ A J 6
```

West	North	East	South
			1NT (15-17)
pass	6NT	all pass	

Your partner leads the ♠K against 6NT and South allows this card to win. By doing so he removes an extra card from your hand in the hope that you will come under pressure later. Declarer wins the second spade with the ace and plays four rounds of clubs. Should you throw a heart or a diamond?

You cannot tell whether South holds four hearts or four diamonds. If you held J-10-x-x in both suits it would be a complete guess which stopper to keep. Here, however, your hearts are stronger than your diamonds and will definitely provide a stopper if South does hold four hearts. The same is not true for your diamond holding. Suppose this is the lie of the diamond suit:

```
               ♦ A K 4
                ┌─────┐
  ♦ J 6         │     │        ♦ 10 7 5 3
                └─────┘
               ♦ Q 9 8 2
```

When declarer plays the ace and king, dropping West's jack on the second round, he will probably finesse the nine next. It is the correct play.

You should therefore discard from your weaker suit (diamonds). You have no idea whether declarer holds four hearts or four diamonds but you do know that the hearts are more likely to be useful as a guard.

If 'discard from your weakest suit' was all you needed to know about discarding, defense would be a good deal easier than it actually is. Let's see some situations where you should ignore this guideline.

Retaining a weak suit because it has been bid

When a four-card suit is visible in the dummy you know you may need to keep a guard on it. The same is true when declarer has bid a suit.

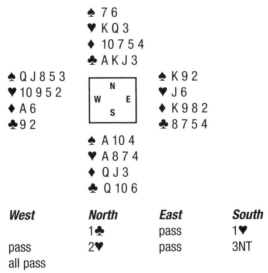

```
                    ♠ 7 6
                    ♥ K Q 3
                    ♦ 10 7 5 4
                    ♣ A K J 3
  ♠ Q J 8 5 3                        ♠ K 9 2
  ♥ 10 9 5 2        ┌───────┐        ♥ J 6
  ♦ A 6             │   N   │        ♦ K 9 8 2
  ♣ 9 2             │ W   E │        ♣ 8 7 5 4
                    │   S   │
                    └───────┘
                    ♠ A 10 4
                    ♥ A 8 7 4
                    ♦ Q J 3
                    ♣ Q 10 6
```

West	North	East	South
	1♣	pass	1♥
pass	2♥	pass	3NT
all pass			

Sitting West, you lead the ♠5 against 3NT and declarer holds up the ace until the third round, throwing a diamond from dummy. Declarer is in no hurry to test for a 3-3 heart break or to play on diamonds in the hope that East (the safe hand) holds both the ace and king. In case something good happens, he prefers to play off four rounds of clubs. You have one easy discard, the ♦6. What should you throw next?

This is not the moment to 'discard from your weakest suit', your four modest hearts. South bid hearts and will therefore hold at least four cards in the suit. He is very likely to hold the ace of hearts. If he holds the jack of hearts too, he will have nine certain tricks, so you must hope that East holds that card. In that case, your 10-9-x-x in hearts will be a stopper in the suit. On the last club you must throw away a spade winner. Declarer has no counter to this defense. If he plays three rounds of hearts, hoping for an even break, your hand will become high. If instead he plays on diamonds, you will win with the ace, cash your remaining spade winner and exit with a low heart. Declarer will lose three spades and two diamonds. One down!

Retaining a guard because partner guards another suit

Sometimes you must keep the weaker of two potential guards because you can deduce (or must hope) that your partner guards the other suit. The key deduction is fairly easy to make on this deal:

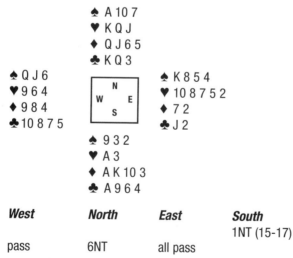

West	North	East	South
			1NT (15-17)
pass	6NT	all pass	

A small slam in diamonds would have been a better contract but the opponents give you a chance by settling in 6NT. Take the West cards for the moment. Seeking a safe lead, as generally recommended against 6NT, you lead the ♦9. Declarer plays four rounds of diamonds, your partner throwing two hearts. You mark time by throwing a heart on the fourth diamond and declarer then plays three rounds of hearts. This is the position as the last heart is led:

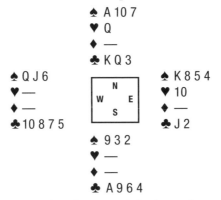

East follows to the last heart and declarer throws a spade. How do you calculate what to throw from the West hand?

The first inference to make is that declarer must hold the ace of clubs. His play so far would be nonsense if he were missing that card. He would obviously have knocked out the ace of clubs before cashing his three heart winners. The next question to ask is: who holds the king of spades? There are two solid reasons why you should place your partner with this card. Can you think of them?

The first reason is that South's opening 1NT bid promised 15-17 points. You have already deduced that he must hold the ace of clubs and that will give him fifteen points outside spades. The spade king in addition would carry him over the top for a 1NT opening. The second reason — equally powerful — is that if declarer does hold the king of spades he will have twelve tricks! He will have seven tricks in the red suits — already banked — three top clubs and two top spades.

Once you have placed partner with the king of spades, it is an easy matter to decide what to discard. You throw the ♠6 and declarer is doomed. He will cross his fingers and play on the club suit but your 10-8-7-5 will spoil his day. One down!

Retaining a guard on the threat you can see

Sometimes it seems that you hold two critical guards and will give away the contract whatever you throw. If that is in fact the case, you will have to surrender gracefully and congratulate the declarer. Perhaps, though, he does not have the cards you fear and you can safely discard from one of your holdings. In this situation it is vital to retain the guard on the threat you can actually see (the one in dummy). Take the West cards here:

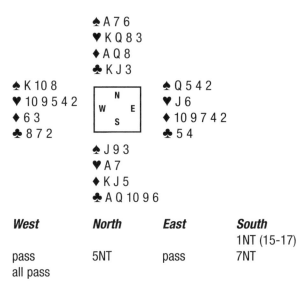

West	**North**	**East**	**South**
			1NT (15-17)
pass	5NT	pass	7NT
all pass			

North's 5NT asks partner to bid either 6NT or 7NT, according to his strength. Looking favorably on his club suit, South ventures the grand slam. Declarer wins your passive club lead and plays three rounds of diamonds. He then surprises you somewhat by cashing the ♠A. When he continues with more clubs you must find a final discard on the fifth club in this end position.

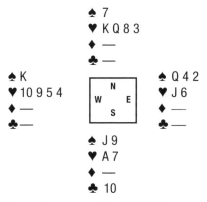

What should you throw on the ♣10? You suspect that declarer holds the ♠Q and that a discard of your ♠K will give him a twelfth trick. *If that is the case, there is nothing you can do about it.* It is your duty to guard the threat you can see — dummy's fourth heart. You must throw the spade king and prepare to congratulate declarer if he does hold the ♠Q and has in fact squeezed you.

As the cards lie, it will be your partner who congratulates you!

Summary

✓ When there is no way of knowing which four-card suits the hidden hand has, it is best to discard from your weakest suit. That's because your cards there are less likely to constitute a guard.

✓ You should try to retain guards in any suit you can see in dummy and in any suit that declarer has bid.

✓ When you think you are squeezed (you hold the sole guard in two suits and must make a discard), retain the guard against the threat you can actually see in the dummy. Declarer may not hold the card you fear.

DISCARD FROM YOUR WEAKEST SUIT

NOW TRY THESE...

1)

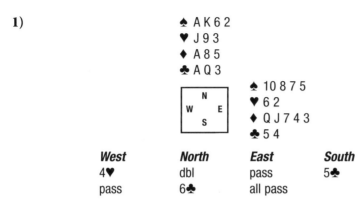

	♠ A K 6 2	
	♥ J 9 3	
	♦ A 8 5	
	♣ A Q 3	

		♠ 10 8 7 5
		♥ 6 2
		♦ Q J 7 4 3
		♣ 5 4

West	North	East	South
4♥	dbl	pass	5♣
pass	6♣	all pass	

Your partner plays the king and ace of hearts, South ruffing the second round. Declarer now runs the trump suit, your partner showing out on the second round. You can afford to throw two diamonds. What will you throw on the next two rounds of trumps?

2)

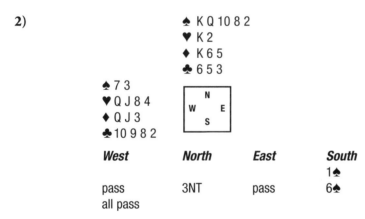

	♠ K Q 10 8 2	
	♥ K 2	
	♦ K 6 5	
	♣ 6 5 3	

| ♠ 7 3 |
| ♥ Q J 8 4 |
| ♦ Q J 3 |
| ♣ 10 9 8 2 |

West	North	East	South
			1♠
pass	3NT	pass	6♠
all pass			

North's 3NT showed a sound raise to 4♠. You lead the ♣10 to your partner's ace, the jack falling from declarer. Partner returns the ♣7 to South's ♣K. Declarer now plays five rounds of spades, your partner showing out on the second round. How do the clubs lie? What should you discard and why?

ANSWERS

1) You cannot afford to throw a spade. If declarer holds a doubleton spade, he will be able to ruff dummy's fourth spade good. If instead he holds Q-x-x or J-x-x, a spade discard will allow him to score four tricks in the suit. You should continue to throw diamonds, hoping that your partner can guard the suit. This may be the whole deal:

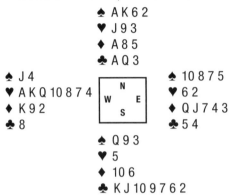

If instead declarer holds something like ♠9-3 ♦ K-9-6, a squeeze is certain.

2) If your partner had started with ♣A-Q-7-4 he would have returned the ♣4 on the second round. So, declarer started with K-Q-J bare and you can safely throw your clubs. Eventually you will have to decide which red suit to throw. Can you see any clue to guide you? If declarer held something like A-10-x in the heart suit, he would have ruffed a heart in dummy instead of running the trumps! This inference allows you to throw your heart guard too, retaining the diamonds. The full deal may look like this:

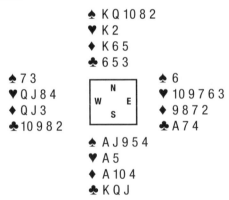

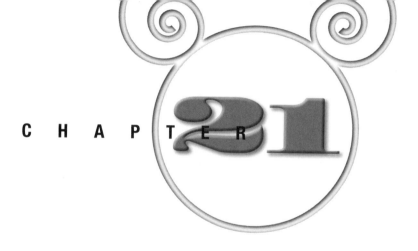

RUFF WHEN YOU CAN

 With most players the desire to make a small trump is very strong.
J.B. Elwell

Playing in a trump contract, rather than in notrump, carries several advantages for declarer. A minor disadvantage is that the defenders can sometimes score ruffs themselves. Usually this is good business for the defenders. They kill one of declarer's winners and score a low trump that would otherwise be useless. This is obvious enough and does not merit an example hand. Let's move straight away to some situations where a defender has a chance to ruff but should look the other way in superior fashion, discarding instead.

Ruffing would cost a trump trick

It is hardly ever right to ruff one of declarer's losing cards when you would consume what would otherwise be a natural trump trick. Let's see an example of this:

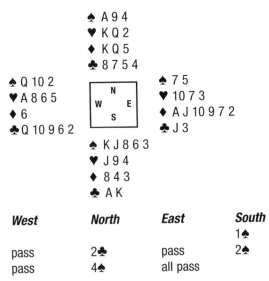

```
                    ♠ A 9 4
                    ♥ K Q 2
                    ♦ K Q 5
                    ♣ 8 7 5 4
   ♠ Q 10 2                      ♠ 7 5
   ♥ A 8 6 5        ┌─────┐      ♥ 10 7 3
   ♦ 6              │  N  │      ♦ A J 10 9 7 2
   ♣ Q 10 9 6 2     │ W E │      ♣ J 3
                    │  S  │
                    └─────┘
                    ♠ K J 8 6 3
                    ♥ J 9 4
                    ♦ 8 4 3
                    ♣ A K
```

West	North	East	South
			1♠
pass	2♣	pass	2♠
pass	4♠	all pass	

Sitting West, you lead your singleton diamond. Partner wins dummy's king of diamonds with the ace and returns the jack of diamonds, declarer following with a low card. What will you do?

It is not at all attractive to ruff one of declarer's losers (a low diamond), when this will kill the natural trump trick that you were expecting. Let's see what happens if you succumb to temptation and ruff. Declarer will eventually lose just three tricks, the two red aces and your diamond ruff.

Suppose instead that you refuse to ruff, throwing a club or a heart. There is nothing declarer can do then. You will score one trump trick and the heart ace; your partner will eventually score a second diamond trick to go with his ace.

The situation would have been different if your partner had held a quick card of re-entry, since you would then have been able to score two ruffs. Let's tweak that last deal a bit:

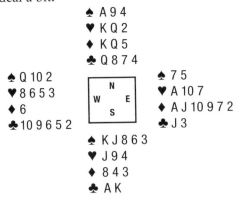

```
                    ♠ A 9 4
                    ♥ K Q 2
                    ♦ K Q 5
                    ♣ Q 8 7 4
   ♠ Q 10 2                      ♠ 7 5
   ♥ 8 6 5 3        ┌─────┐      ♥ A 10 7
   ♦ 6              │  N  │      ♦ A J 10 9 7 2
   ♣ 10 9 6 5 2     │ W E │      ♣ J 3
                    │  S  │
                    └─────┘
                    ♠ K J 8 6 3
                    ♥ J 9 4
                    ♦ 8 4 3
                    ♣ A K
```

Once again you lead your singleton diamond against South's four spades. Partner takes the king with the ace and returns the jack of diamonds. The only winning defense is to ruff the second diamond, cross to partner's hand with the ace of hearts and receive a second diamond ruff. If instead you discard on the second diamond, declarer will win in the dummy and play a trump to the king. After playing the ace and king of clubs, he will return to dummy with the ace of trumps and discard his last diamond on the club queen.

Sometimes when you ruff, declarer is poised to over-ruff. In that situation you must be careful that the ruff does not cost you a natural trump trick. Take the East cards on this slam deal:

```
                    ♠ A K
                    ♥ A 10 7 4
                    ♦ A K Q 5 2
                    ♣ 7 2
  ♠ 10 9 8 6 2              ♠ Q 5 4
  ♥ Q 8           N         ♥ J 6 3
  ♦ J 9 7 6    W     E      ♦ 10 3
  ♣ K 3           S         ♣ Q 10 9 8 4
                    ♠ J 7 3
                    ♥ K 9 5 2
                    ♦ 8 4
                    ♣ A J 6 5
```

West	North	East	South
	1♦	pass	1♥
pass	2♠	pass	2NT
pass	3♥	pass	4♣
pass	6♥	all pass	

Your partner leads the ♠10 against South's small slam in hearts. Declarer wins with dummy's ♠A and, somewhat mysteriously, plays the three top diamonds. Can you work out what is happening? How will you defend?

When the deal arose at the table East decided to ruff the third diamond with the ♥3. Declarer overruffed, drew trumps in two rounds and claimed the contract. He had one trump left in his hand, to ruff the diamonds good, and the only remaining loser in dummy would be a small club. Slam made!

East should have seen through declarer's cunning plan. If his trumps were solid he would surely have drawn trumps before playing on diamonds. If his trumps were not solid, then East's J-6-3 was a valuable holding worth preserving. As you see, if East declines to ruff, declarer cannot avoid one trump loser and a further loser in clubs.

Ruffing will allow declarer to draw trumps ending in the dummy

West had to resist the urge to ruff on the next deal too. The reason for doing so was quite different.

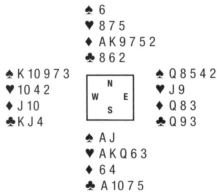

```
                    ♠ 6
                    ♥ 8 7 5
                    ♦ A K 9 7 5 2
                    ♣ 8 6 2
   ♠ K 10 9 7 3                      ♠ Q 8 5 4 2
   ♥ 10 4 2          N               ♥ J 9
   ♦ J 10        W        E          ♦ Q 8 3
   ♣ K J 4          S               ♣ Q 9 3
                    ♠ A J
                    ♥ A K Q 6 3
                    ♦ 6 4
                    ♣ A 10 7 5
```

South arrived in 6♥. It may seem an ambitious contract but on a trump lead it would have been an easy make. Declarer would draw trumps and duck a diamond to set up dummy's suit. Take the West cards and suppose that you lead the ♦J, which happens to prevent declarer from ducking a diamond later. South wins with the ace of diamonds, cashes the diamond king and ruffs a third round of diamonds with the ♥3. How should you defend?

It may seem natural to overruff with the ♥4, scoring a trump trick that you did not expect to make. To do so will prove fatal. Declarer will win your return and draw the outstanding trumps with the ace and king. He will then play the ♠A and cross to dummy by ruffing the spade jack. Dummy's good diamonds will then allow him to throw all three club losers! It was not difficult to predict this outcome, nor to see how to thwart declarer's plan. If you refuse to overruff, maintaining your trump length, declarer will not be able to draw trumps and cross to dummy with a spade ruff. You will never make a trump trick, it's true, but the slam will go down. Declarer will have no way to swallow his club losers.

Overruffing would stop your side promoting a trump

When you are in a position to overruff the declarer you should never rush your decision. By refusing to overruff, you may find that you are promoting a second trump trick for your side. On the next deal this is obvious:

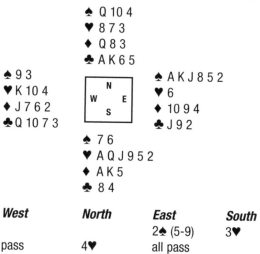

```
                    ♠ Q 10 4
                    ♥ 8 7 3
                    ♦ Q 8 3
                    ♣ A K 6 5
    ♠ 9 3                           ♠ A K J 8 5 2
    ♥ K 10 4         N              ♥ 6
    ♦ J 7 6 2     W     E           ♦ 10 9 4
    ♣ Q 10 7 3       S              ♣ J 9 2
                    ♠ 7 6
                    ♥ A Q J 9 5 2
                    ♦ A K 5
                    ♣ 8 4
```

West	North	East	South
		2♠ (5-9)	3♥
pass	4♥	all pass	

Sitting West, you lead the ♠9 against South's game in hearts. Your partner scores two winners in the suit and returns a third spade. What should you do if declarer ruffs with the queen?

If you overruff with the king, declarer's A-J of trumps will pick up your remaining 10-4. You will score only one trump trick and the contract will be made. Overruffing would be poor defense because you can see that if you discard instead you will be left with two certain trump tricks. Your K-10-4 will sit over declarer's remaining A-J-9.

BY THE WAY

There is more to this deal than meets the eye. Against an expert declarer you would have to discard specifically a club to beat the contract. Suppose you throw a diamond instead. Declarer can cash the two top clubs and ruff a club. He can then play three rounds of diamonds and ruff another club. This would leave him with just three cards in his hand: A-J-9 of trumps to your K-10-4. He could then exit with the ♥9, forcing you to win and lead back into his tenace.

Summary

✓ Scoring a ruff in defense is usually an extra trick. Be wary of ruffing when this may give declarer access (by way of the trump suit) to a long side suit in dummy.

✓ Do not overruff the declarer when there is any chance that you may promote a trump trick for your side by refusing to overruff.

RUFF WHEN YOU CAN

1)

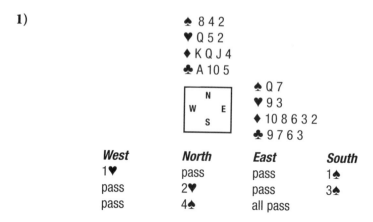

	♠ 8 4 2		
	♥ Q 5 2		
	♦ K Q J 4		
	♣ A 10 5		

♠ Q 7
♥ 9 3
♦ 10 8 6 3 2
♣ 9 7 6 3

West	North	East	South
1♥	pass	pass	1♠
pass	2♥	pass	3♠
pass	4♠	all pass	

Your partner plays the king and ace of hearts, South following with the four and eight. At Trick 3 partner plays the ♥J, covered by dummy's queen. Will you ruff? If so, which card will you use for the ruff?

2)

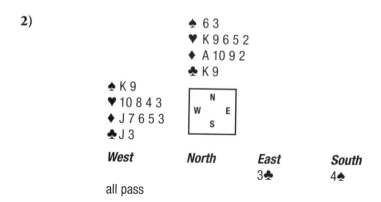

	♠ 6 3		
	♥ K 9 6 5 2		
	♦ A 10 9 2		
	♣ K 9		

♠ K 9
♥ 10 8 4 3
♦ J 7 6 5 3
♣ J 3

West	North	East	South
		3♣	4♠
all pass			

You lead the ♣J against South's spade game and your partner scores two tricks with the ace and queen. At Trick 3 your partner continues with another club, declarer ruffing with the jack. Will you overruff or not? What is the reason for your decision?

ANSWERS

1) Not only should you ruff the third round of hearts, you should ruff with the queen in the hope of promoting a trump trick for partner. This may be the full deal:

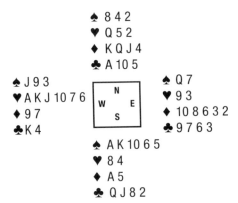

```
                    ♠ 8 4 2
                    ♥ Q 5 2
                    ♦ K Q J 4
                    ♣ A 10 5
    ♠ J 9 3                        ♠ Q 7
    ♥ A K J 10 7 6   N            ♥ 9 3
    ♦ 9 7         W     E         ♦ 10 8 6 3 2
    ♣ K 4            S            ♣ 9 7 6 3
                    ♠ A K 10 6 5
                    ♥ 8 4
                    ♦ A 5
                    ♣ Q J 8 2
```

When you ruff with the queen, declarer cannot avoid the loss of two trump tricks. Another possibility is that your partner holds a minor-suit winner and only J-x in the trump suit (which will be promoted when you ruff with the queen). Even if partner holds only five hearts it cannot cost you to take the ruff with the queen.

2) You should not overruff. With so many high cards in the dummy it is almost certain that you need two trump tricks to beat the contract. Suppose declarer started with A-Q-J-8-7-5 in the trump suit. If you over-ruff the jack with the king, he can win your return and cash the ace of trumps to drop your nine. He can then cross to dummy to finesse against your partner's remaining 10-x. Refuse to overruff instead and there is a good chance that declarer will cross to dummy to finesse the ♠Q. Your side will then score two trump tricks.

Another possibility is that declarer's trumps are A-J-10-8-7-5. If you over-ruff the jack with the king, declarer will subsequently cross to dummy for a finesse of the ten. When this drops your nine, he can return to dummy and pick up your partner's remaining Q-x with a finesse of the eight. If instead you refuse to overruff, declarer must lose two trump tricks.

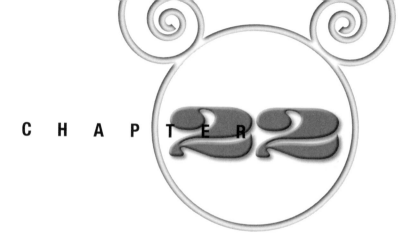

CHAPTER 22

NEVER GIVE A
RUFF-AND-SLUFF

 It is bad play to lead a suit that both the declarer and the dummy can trump. It allows declarer to trump in one hand and to discard a worthless card from the other. *J.B. Elwell*

What would you say was the biggest gaffe you can make in defense? Ruffing your partner's ace is probably the worst (although even that can be good play sometimes!). Also riding high in the list is to give a ruff-and-sluff. In other words, you lead a suit where both declarer and the dummy are void. This allows declarer to ruff in one hand and dispose of a loser from the other. Most of the time it will cost you a trick.

Let's see a typical example of a defender making such a mistake.

```
              ♠ J 9 7 4
              ♥ A 8
              ♦ 10 9 3
              ♣ K Q 7 2
♠ Q 6 2                      ♠ 3
♥ J 10 9 4       N           ♥ Q 6 5 3 2
♦ K 8 6       W     E        ♦ Q 7 5 4 2
♣ 10 8 5         S           ♣ 9 4
              ♠ A K 10 8 5
              ♥ K 7
              ♦ A J
              ♣ A J 6 3
```

West leads the ♥J against a small slam in spades. Declarer wins with the ace and plays two rounds of trumps, not pleased to see that he has a loser in the suit. Hoping for a defensive mistake, he cashes the king of hearts and plays three rounds of clubs. West is then thrown on lead with a trump. What should he do now, do you think?

Fearful that declarer holds the ♦A-Q, many defenders would play a third round of hearts. Mistake! Declarer will ruff in the dummy and discard the diamond loser from his hand, making the slam.

"I was hoping that declarer had another heart," West will explain to his partner. It is not a good excuse. If declarer had a third heart he would have ruffed it in dummy before throwing West in. The only chance of beating the contract was a diamond switch away from the king. If East holds the diamond queen that will be one down. If South holds A-Q in the suit the slam was unbeatable anyway.

Ruff-and-sluff that does not give up a trick

It often happens that a defender is on lead and must choose between conceding a ruff-and-sluff and making the first play in a new suit, which will perhaps give declarer a trick. On the deal we have just seen, the ruff-and-sluff would be costly, so West had to risk opening a new suit. Sometimes it is correct to give a ruff-and-sluff. Look at this deal:

```
              ♠ A 8
              ♥ A 8 5 3
              ♦ A 9 7 2
              ♣ J 6 5
♠ Q J 10 2         N          ♠ K 9 7 6 5 3
♥ 9 2          W       E      ♥ 6 4
♦ Q 10 3           S          ♦ 8 5
♣ Q 9 8 4                     ♣ 10 7 2
              ♠ 4
              ♥ K Q J 10 7
              ♦ K J 6 4
              ♣ A K 3
```

South arrives in 6♥ and you lead the ♠Q, won with dummy's ace. Declarer draws trumps in two rounds, ruffs dummy's last spade and plays ace, king and another club, putting you on lead. What should you do?

If you play a spade or a club you will give declarer a ruff-and-sluff. Many defenders would conclude their analysis there, switching to a diamond in the hope that East holds the diamond jack. The slam will then be made. Instead you should count declarer's distribution. He started with one spade, five hearts and three clubs. How many diamonds does that leave him? Four! A ruff-and-sluff will not help him. He can throw away the fourth diamond, from one hand or other, but will still have a diamond loser on the third round of the suit. So, you must steel yourself to give declarer a ruff-and-sluff. Beating the slam will be your reward.

Ruff-and-sluff to promote a trump trick

One way in which the defenders can promote a trump trick is known as the 'uppercut'. By ruffing with his highest trump a defender forces a trump honor from declarer, thereby promoting the other defender's trumps.

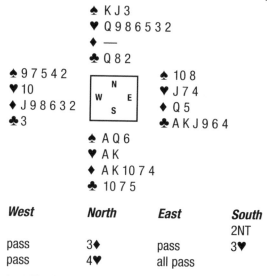

♠ K J 3
♥ Q 9 8 6 5 3 2
♦ —
♣ Q 8 2

♠ 9 7 5 4 2
♥ 10
♦ J 9 8 6 3 2
♣ 3

♠ 10 8
♥ J 7 4
♦ Q 5
♣ A K J 9 6 4

♠ A Q 6
♥ A K
♦ A K 10 7 4
♣ 10 7 5

West	North	East	South
			2NT
pass	3♦	pass	3♥
pass	4♥	all pass	

South plays in 4♥ after a transfer auction and West leads the ♣3. Take the East cards now. What should you do after scoring three clubs?

South's 2NT opening bid marks him with the outstanding high cards. The only chance of another defensive trick lies in the trump suit. You lead a fourth round of clubs, giving a ruff-and-sluff, and the declarer has no resource. If he ruffs with the ace or king, your jack of trumps will be promoted. Suppose instead that South discards a spade. Your partner will ruff with his ♥10 to force dummy's queen. Once again you will make a trick with your jack of trumps.

Ruff-and-sluff to prepare for a trump promotion

Occasionally you need to give declarer a ruff-and-sluff in order to prepare for a trump promotion.

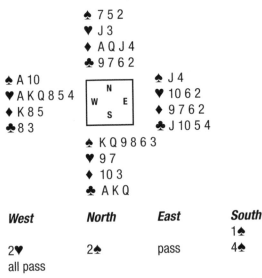

♠ 7 5 2
♥ J 3
♦ A Q J 4
♣ 9 7 6 2

♠ A 10
♥ A K Q 8 5 4
♦ K 8 5
♣ 8 3

N
W   E
S

♠ J 4
♥ 10 6 2
♦ 9 7 6 2
♣ J 10 5 4

♠ K Q 9 8 6 3
♥ 9 7
♦ 10 3
♣ A K Q

West	North	East	South
			1♠
2♥	2♠	pass	4♠
all pass			

Sitting West, you lead the ♥K to request a count signal. Partner's ♥2 shows an odd number of hearts. How can you beat the contract?

Partner surely holds three hearts, so you can see three major-suit winners for yourself. Your ♦K is doomed under the dummy's holding and declarer's strong bidding surely implies that he has no club losers. The only remaining chance is to score two trump tricks. This can be done if partner holds jack doubleton and can ruff the fourth round of hearts.

You cash the ♥A and continue with a third round, giving declarer a ruff-and-sluff. Partner may give you a dirty look but — just for once — you know what you are doing! Let's say that declarer ruffs in the dummy and discards a diamond. When he continues with a trump to the king you win with the ace and lead yet another heart. Partner ruffs with the jack, forcing declarer's queen, and your ♠10 is promoted into the setting trick.

Summary

✓ Giving declarer a ruff-and-sluff is generally a bad idea. Declarer can ruff in one hand and dispose of a card that would otherwise be a loser from the other hand.

✓ When you must either give a ruff-and-sluff or make the first play in a new suit, try to work out whether the ruff-and-sluff will be useful to declarer. If it will, you may have to risk playing the new suit.

N E V E R   G I V E   A   R U F F - A N D - S L U F F

NOW TRY THESE...

1)

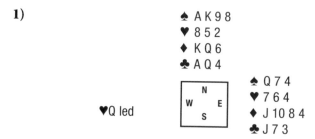

♥Q led

```
            ♠ A K 9 8
            ♥ 8 5 2
            ♦ K Q 6
            ♣ A Q 4
                        ♠ Q 7 4
                        ♥ 7 6 4
                        ♦ J 10 8 4
                        ♣ J 7 3
```

South, who opened 1♠, is now playing in 6♠. He wins the opening lead with the ♥A and draws two rounds of trumps, your partner throwing a heart on the second round. He continues with a heart to the king, the A-K-Q of diamonds, everyone following three times, and a heart ruff in his hand. With the red suits eliminated, he then puts you on lead with the ♠Q. What will you return?

2)

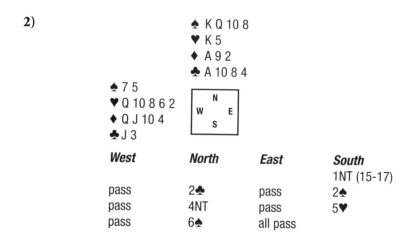

```
            ♠ K Q 10 8
            ♥ K 5
            ♦ A 9 2
            ♣ A 10 8 4
♠ 7 5
♥ Q 10 8 6 2
♦ Q J 10 4
♣ J 3
```

West	North	East	South
			1NT (15-17)
pass	2♣	pass	2♠
pass	4NT	pass	5♥
pass	6♠	all pass	

South wins your ♦Q lead with his king. After drawing trumps in three rounds, your partner following with small cards, declarer cashes the ace and king of hearts (your partner playing high-low to show an even number of cards in the suit). Declarer then plays the ♦A followed by a low diamond, partner following twice more. What shape is declarer's hand? What will you play next?

ANSWERS

1) Should you give a ruff-and-sluff or lead a club into dummy's A-Q? You should play a club. Partner doubtless holds the ♣K but declarer could have taken the club finesse anyway. A club from you will not help him in the slightest. If instead you concede a ruff-and-sluff, declarer will ruff in his hand and throw the ♣4 from dummy. A subsequent finesse of the ♣Q will succeed, leaving him with no club losers. This is the full deal:

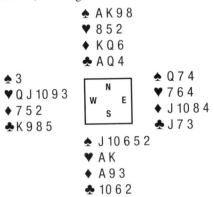

2) You know from your partner's echo that declarer has either four hearts or two. With four hearts, he would have responded 2♥ to the Stayman inquiry, so you can assume he has two and 4-2-3-4 shape. Since he holds four clubs in each hand, a ruff-and-sluff will not help him. Exiting with a club instead will allow declarer to avoid a club loser if the deal is:

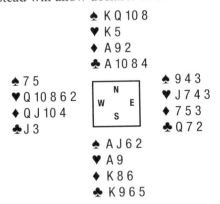

If you exit with the ♣J, declarer can win with the ace in the dummy and finesse his ♣9. If you exit with the ♣3 instead, declarer will win partner's queen with the king and your jack will show up on the next club lead.

CHAPTER 23

SPLIT YOUR HONORS

 If you have two honors in sequence, and the hand over you be in a position to overtake any card you play, the lower honor should be played. *J.B. Elwell*

In Chapter 17 we saw that you should split honors (play one of touching, or near-touching, honors) in a situation such as this:

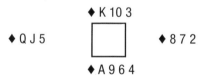

When a low diamond is led from the South hand, you must insert the queen or jack to stop declarer finessing the ten.

The same play would be necessary, of course, if the North and South hands were reversed and the initial lead was made from dummy:

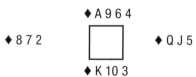

When the ♦4 is led from dummy you cannot see declarer's K-10-3. Nothing much can be lost by playing an honor, though, and you should do so in case declarer does hold the ten with his king.

Another reason to split honors is to prevent declarer from ducking the trick into your partner's hand. Take the East cards on this deal:

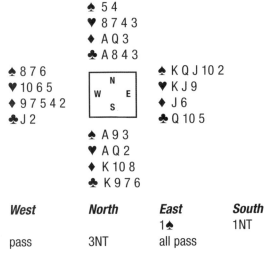

♠ 5 4
♥ 8 7 4 3
♦ A Q 3
♣ A 8 4 3

♠ 8 7 6　　　　♠ K Q J 10 2
♥ 10 6 5　　　　♥ K J 9
♦ 9 7 5 4 2　　♦ J 6
♣ J 2　　　　　♣ Q 10 5

♠ A 9 3
♥ A Q 2
♦ K 10 8
♣ K 9 7 6

West	North	East	South
		1♠	1NT
pass	3NT	all pass	

Partner leads a spade and you persist with the suit, South winning the third round. Declarer crosses to dummy with the ♦Q and leads a low club. What is your reaction, sitting East?

If you play the ♣5, declarer will cover gratefully with the six, ducking a club trick into the safe hand. Your partner has no spade to return, so declarer will be able to claim nine tricks when he regains the lead and finds that the clubs started 3-2. To prevent declarer ducking the club to your partner you must insert the ♣10 on the first round. He will have to win with the king and will no doubt continue with ace and another club (nothing else is better). When you turn up with the long club and cash two more spades, the contract is one down.

Now it's time to look at some situations where splitting your honors can be the wrong thing to do.

Splitting honors might crash partner's honor

When partner might hold a bare honor you must be wary of contributing a further honor to the trick yourself.

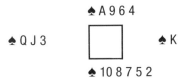

♠A 9 6 4

♠Q J 3　　　　　　　　♠ K

♠ 10 8 7 5 2

Suppose declarer is in 6♠ with this trump holding. Needing a 2-2 break in the suit, he leads the ♠2 from the South hand. If you split your honors, declarer will win with the ace and your partner's king will complete an expensive trick. What is worse, every member of the club will hear the story before nightfall!

Why is it wrong to split your honors here? Often you will know from the bidding that declarer has five trumps. With something like K-10-x-x-x in his hand he will have no intention of taking a first-round finesse. Play the three and he will surely rise with dummy's ace, later losing a trump trick.

Splitting honors might save declarer a guess

Suppose declarer needs two tricks from this diamond side suit:

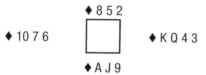

He leads a low diamond from dummy, with the intention of playing the nine. (This is the best play because it gains against K-10 or Q-10 with East; finessing the jack gains only against K-Q with East.) If you split your honors, inserting the queen, declarer may reassess the situation. He may win with the ace and lead towards the jack, scoring two tricks in the suit.

If declarer actually held A-J-10 he would score two tricks however you defended.

It is particularly expensive to split your honors in this situation:

When declarer leads a low spade from the South hand, you will see some defenders inserting an honor! What possible advantage can there be in this? Declarer wins with dummy's ace and sees East show out. He returns to his hand in another suit and can then pick up the suit by finessing dummy's ten. Play a sensible ♠4 on the first round instead and declarer will surely rise with dummy's ace. The same is true when South holds five small spades instead of six. When you play low declarer has no reason to take a finesse.

BY THE WAY

If declarer held K-10-x-x-x opposite A-9-x-x in the trump suit and no losers in the side suits, he might indeed take a first-round finesse of dummy's ♠9 as a safety play against a 4-0 trump break. This is still no justification for you to split your Q-J-x since the slam would make anyway.

BY THE WAY

Suppose East held ♦ K-10-x or ♦ Q-10-x, again with three small diamonds in dummy. Some players would insert their top honor on the first round as a bluff. They would hope to convey the impression of K-Q-x, thereby diverting a declarer with A-J-9 from the percentage play!

BY THE WAY

Some tricksters would insert the queen from Q-x, sitting West in this situation. They hope that declarer has five small cards in the suit and will read them for Q-J-x, finessing into partner's original J-x on the second round! If you attempt this deception and it works, do not smile too brightly. It means that declarer rated you silly enough to split a Q-J-x holding!

Summary

✓ Split your honors when there is a chance that declarer will otherwise finesse a lower card sitting over you, depriving you of a trick in the suit.

✓ Do not split your honors when there is a risk that partner has a bare honor and that you will crash honors.

✓ Do not split your honors when this may assist declarer with a guess in the suit.

SPLIT YOUR HONORS

NOW TRY THESE...

1)

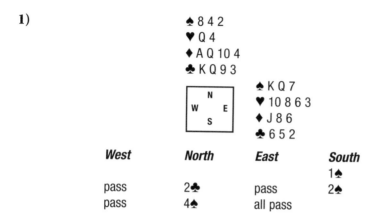

♠ 8 4 2
♥ Q 4
♦ A Q 10 4
♣ K Q 9 3

♠ K Q 7
♥ 10 8 6 3
♦ J 8 6
♣ 6 5 2

West	North	East	South
			1♠
pass	2♣	pass	2♠
pass	4♠	all pass	

Your partner cashes the king and ace of hearts. You signal an even number of cards in the suit and declarer follows with the jack on the second round. When partner switches to the ♦7, declarer wins with dummy's ace and leads a low spade from the dummy. Will you split your honors or not? What is the reason for your decision?

2)

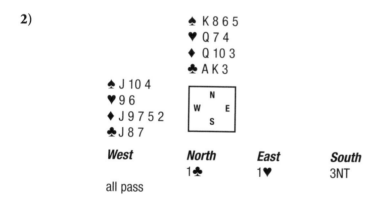

♠ K 8 6 5
♥ Q 7 4
♦ Q 10 3
♣ A K 3

♠ J 10 4
♥ 9 6
♦ J 9 7 5 2
♣ J 8 7

West	North	East	South
	1♣	1♥	3NT
all pass			

You lead the ♥9 and declarer wins with the ace. He then leads the ♠3 from the South hand. Will you split your honors or not? What is the reason for your decision?

ANSWERS

1) You should not split your honors. This would cost the contract if declarer held A-10-9 sixth and your partner had a singleton jack. By playing low you would ensure two trump tricks for the defense. Another possibility is that declarer holds A-J-9-x-x(-x) in the trump suit. If you play low, he may well try the nine and lose to your partner's ten.

2) You should split your honors, inserting the ♠J. Perhaps the whole deal looks like this:

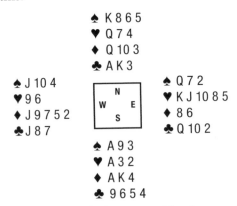

                ♠ K 8 6 5
                ♥ Q 7 4
                ♦ Q 10 3
                ♣ A K 3

♠ J 10 4   ♠ Q 7 2
♥ 9 6   ♥ K J 10 8 5
♦ J 9 7 5 2   ♦ 8 6
♣ J 8 7   ♣ Q 10 2

                ♠ A 9 3
                ♥ A 3 2
                ♦ A K 4
                ♣ 9 6 5 4

Declarer wins the ♥9 with the ace and leads a spade, hoping to duck the trick to the safe (East) hand and then to find a 3-3 spade break. You prevent this by inserting the jack and declarer wins with dummy's king. On this trick your partner must continue the good work by discarding his queen (otherwise he will have to win the second or third round of spades). Declarer cannot safely develop the spade suit now. If he plays ace, king and another club instead, your partner must ditch the other black queen on one of the first two rounds! You will then be able to win the third round of clubs and play a heart through dummy's queen.

Yes, as the cards lie, declarer could have made the contract by holding up the ♥A for one round, and winning the second round. He could then have ducked a round of spades to you, sitting West, and you would have had no heart to return. Even better, North-South could have bid differently, arranging for North to be the declarer in 3NT.

FOLLOW LOW
WHEN A TRICK IS LOST

 To be able to use proper judgement in ridding yourself of cards that you fear may block your partner's suit, you should have perfect confidence that your partner has made the correct lead. **J.B. Elwell**

Back in Chapter 14 we looked at the general rule of playing high in the third seat. The purpose was to attempt to win the trick or at least to drive out a high card from declarer. When dummy has already won the trick there is usually no point in playing your highest card underneath it. It is better to keep whatever honors you hold for subsequent tricks.

                    ♣ A 9 7 5

♣ 8 3   [ ]   ♣ K Q J 2

                    ♣ 10 6 4

    Partner leads the ♣8, won by dummy's ace. If you waste an honor now ("I didn't want to give you a discouraging two, partner!"), declarer will be able to build a second trick in the suit.

    It is sometimes beneficial to play a higher card than necessary under dummy's winner. This is when — for one reason or another — you do not want to win a subsequent trick in the suit. Let's see some of these situations.

Following low would block the suit

When partner has led from an honor combination, it may suit you to unblock from a doubleton honor, so that you can cross to his hand on the second round of the suit. Take the East cards here:

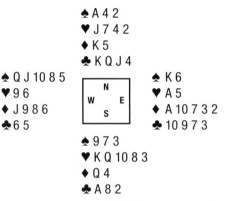

♠ A 4 2
♥ J 7 4 2
♦ K 5
♣ K Q J 4

♠ Q J 10 8 5
♥ 9 6
♦ J 9 8 6
♣ 6 5

♠ K 6
♥ A 5
♦ A 10 7 3 2
♣ 10 9 7 3

♠ 9 7 3
♥ K Q 10 8 3
♦ Q 4
♣ A 8 2

South bids to a game in hearts and your partner leads the ♠Q, won with dummy's ace. Which card should you play?

Suppose you follow with the ♠6, preserving the king to win a later trick. You will soon regret it! When you get the lead with the trump ace, you can cash the ♠K but there will be no route to the second spade winner in partner's hand. Declarer will win your return, draw trumps, and throw his spade loser on the fourth round of clubs.

See how much better the defense goes if you drop your ♠K at Trick 1 under dummy's ace. You will then be able to return your ♠6 to partner's hand. With his present holding he can cash two spade tricks. Even without the ♠10 or ♠9, he could give you a spade ruff.

Here is another deal, played in notrump this time, where you need to unblock in order to maintain communications with partner's hand.

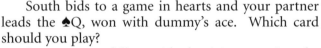

BY THE WAY

Did you notice that declarer could have made that 4♥ contract? He should have ducked the first round of spades. When he wins the second spade and plays a trump to your ace, you will have no route to your partner's hand.

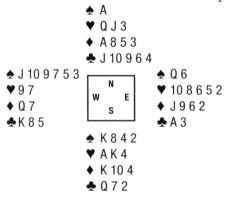

♠ A
♥ Q J 3
♦ A 8 5 3
♣ J 10 9 6 4

♠ J 10 9 7 5 3
♥ 9 7
♦ Q 7
♣ K 8 5

♠ Q 6
♥ 10 8 6 5 2
♦ J 9 6 2
♣ A 3

♠ K 8 4 2
♥ A K 4
♦ K 10 4
♣ Q 7 2

South opens 1NT, raised to 3NT, and your partner leads the ♠J to dummy's ace. Will you play the queen or the six?

Let's see what happens if you follow with the six. When declarer plays a club it will make no difference whether you rise with the ace or not. If you do, declarer will allow your ♣Q to win the next trick. With his spade guard intact, he can then win your return and clear the clubs. If instead you allow partner to win the first round of clubs, your ♣Q will block the suit.

The ♣Q is a liability and you should dispose of it under dummy's ace. When declarer plays on clubs you should jump in with the ace and return the ♠6. Your partner will be able to clear the spade suit and his ♣K will serve as an entry to the long cards.

There are many other situations where you must avoid a blockage:

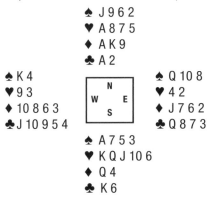

$$♠ A 4$$

♠ 10 8 7 6 2   ♠ K Q J 5

♠ 9 3

Partner leads the ♠6 against a 3NT contract. Seeing no value in a hold-up, declarer rises with dummy's ace. If you fail to unblock an honor, your K-Q-J will block the suit. Whichever defender subsequently gains the lead, your side will be able to claim only three spade tricks.

Following low would allow you to be endplayed

One of the most common forms of endplay is the ruff-and-sluff elimination (where declarer eliminates one or more suits and then throws a defender in). When one of these endings is threatened you must be wary of retaining bare high cards that may enable declarer to throw you in.

```
            ♠ J 9 6 2
            ♥ A 8 7 5
            ♦ A K 9
            ♣ A 2
  ♠ K 4         N          ♠ Q 10 8
  ♥ 9 3      W     E        ♥ 4 2
  ♦ 10 8 6 3     S          ♦ J 7 6 2
  ♣ J 10 9 5 4              ♣ Q 8 7 3
            ♠ A 7 5 3
            ♥ K Q J 10 6
            ♦ Q 4
            ♣ K 6
```

Sitting West, you lead the ♣J against South's small slam in hearts. Declarer wins dummy's ace, draws trumps in two rounds and plays the ♠A. Will you play the four or the king?

Defenders unfamiliar with the situation will follow with the ♠4. Not the best! Declarer will play his other club winner followed by three rounds of

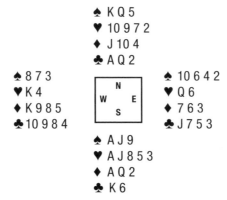

diamonds, throwing a spade. When another spade is played, West will have to win with the bare king. The enforced return of a minor suit will give declarer a ruff-and-sluff, allowing him to throw his last spade loser.

To avoid this endplay you must play the ♠K under declarer's ace. Your partner can then score two spade tricks when the spade exit comes. There is no risk attached to this unblock. If declarer held either A-Q-x-x or A-10-x-x he would be taking finesses in the suit, not cashing the ace.

The same inference is available to the defenders in the trump suit. West handed the opponents a vulnerable slam when this deal arose:

```
              ♠ K Q 5
              ♥ 10 9 7 2
              ♦ J 10 4
              ♣ A Q 2
  ♠ 8 7 3            N          ♠ 10 6 4 2
  ♥ K 4          W       E      ♥ Q 6
  ♦ K 9 8 5          S          ♦ 7 6 3
  ♣ 10 9 8 4                    ♣ J 7 5 3
              ♠ A J 9
              ♥ A J 8 5 3
              ♦ A Q 2
              ♣ K 6
```

South opens 1♥ and soon arrives in a small slam. Sitting West, you lead the ♣10 against six hearts. Declarer wins with dummy's ace of clubs and plays a trump to the ace. If you are half asleep you will follow with the four, of course. Suppose, for the moment, that you are wide awake. Is there any reason to play the king of trumps under South's ace?

There sure is! If you play low, declarer will play the king of clubs next, followed by three rounds of spades ending in the dummy. He will throw one diamond loser on the queen of clubs and then play a second round of trumps. When you win with the bare king of trumps, you will be endplayed. A diamond return will run into South's ace-queen; a club return will give a ruff-and-sluff.

To avoid the endplay you must ditch the king of trumps under declarer's ace. There is no real risk attached to this, since declarer would surely have taken a trump finesse if he held the queen as well as the ace. Declarer will no doubt follow the same line of play, in the hope that you started with K-Q doubleton in the trump suit. When East wins the second round of trumps with the queen, and the slam goes down, there should be a few admiring nods in your direction. If not, you will have to nod admiringly to yourself.

When declarer is developing the tricks he needs, in a notrump contract, he must often take steps to keep the danger hand off lead. As a defender, you can sometimes thwart him by unblocking a high card in order to promote one of partner's cards into an entry. An example will make this clear. Take the East cards and see what you make of this deal:

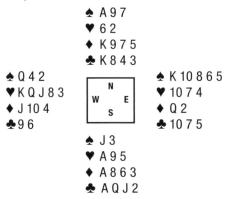

```
                    ♠ A 9 7
                    ♥ 6 2
                    ♦ K 9 7 5
                    ♣ K 8 4 3
    ♠ Q 4 2                          ♠ K 10 8 6 5
    ♥ K Q J 8 3        N             ♥ 10 7 4
    ♦ J 10 4       W       E         ♦ Q 2
    ♣ 9 6              S             ♣ 10 7 5
                    ♠ J 3
                    ♥ A 9 5
                    ♦ A 8 6 3
                    ♣ A Q J 2
```

South opens 1NT, raised to 3NT, and your partner leads the king of hearts. The king wins the first trick and West continues with the queen and jack of hearts, declarer winning the third round. With eight top tricks on view, he now leads a low diamond from his hand. His intention is to play dummy's ♦9, ducking the trick into your hand because you have no heart to play. To prevent this, your partner will rise with the jack of diamonds. Declarer cannot duck now or West will cash his heart tricks. He wins with dummy's king, therefore, and… all depends on what you do in the East seat. Any ideas?

To beat the contract you must play the ♦Q under dummy's ♦K. Declarer cannot then set up a diamond trick without West gaining the lead. The game will go one down. (If declarer tries his luck with four rounds of clubs, West must discard two spades, keeping two good hearts and his diamond guard.)

Summary

✓ When dummy has already won the trick you have a free choice of which card to play. Usually you will not want to expend an honor unnecessarily. You can use your spot-cards for signaling.

✓ One reason to drop an honor under dummy's winner is to avoid a blockage in the suit. When partner's ♥Q lead is won by dummy's ace, for example, you may wish to unblock the king from ♥K-x.

✓ Another reason to unblock an honor is that you fear being thrown in with the honor should you retain it.

FOLLOW LOW WHEN A TRICK IS LOST

NOW TRY THESE...

1)

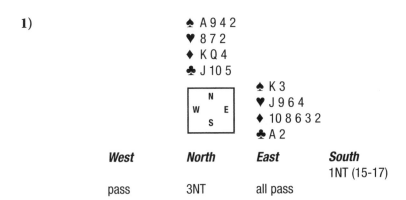

♠ A 9 4 2
♥ 8 7 2
♦ K Q 4
♣ J 10 5

♠ K 3
♥ J 9 6 4
♦ 10 8 6 3 2
♣ A 2

West	North	East	South
			1NT (15-17)
pass	3NT	all pass	

Your partner leads the ♠Q against 3NT and declarer wins with dummy's ace. Which card will you play? How do you expect the play to develop after your chosen play?

2)

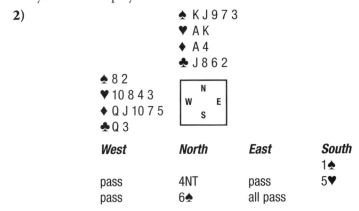

♠ K J 9 7 3
♥ A K
♦ A 4
♣ J 8 6 2

♠ 8 2
♥ 10 8 4 3
♦ Q J 10 7 5
♣ Q 3

West	North	East	South
			1♠
pass	4NT	pass	5♥
pass	6♠	all pass	

You don't think much of North's bidding? Never mind about that! How will you defend? You lead the ♦Q and declarer wins with dummy's ace, partner playing a discouraging ♦2. Declarer now crosses to the ♣A. Will you play the three or the queen? What is the reason for your choice?

ANSWERS

1) I hope you didn't answer this question too quickly! Normally you would unblock the king from K-x because you do not want to block the suit. Here you cannot afford to do so because you can see that dummy's ♠9 will then be promoted into a second stopper. So, you should play your ♠3 on the first round. If declarer plays on clubs next you will rise smartly with the ace and cash your ♠K. The way will then be clear for partner to enjoy his remaining spades, should he gain the lead later.

2) You should dispose of your ♣Q under the ace. Why do you think declarer is playing on clubs before even drawing trumps? It is because he wants to catch you asleep, before his intended endplay becomes obvious. This may be the full deal:

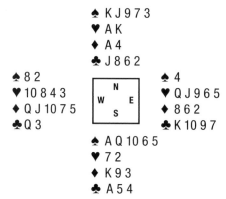

```
              ♠ K J 9 7 3
              ♥ A K
              ♦ A 4
              ♣ J 8 6 2
  ♠ 8 2                      ♠ 4
  ♥ 10 8 4 3      N          ♥ Q J 9 6 5
  ♦ Q J 10 7 5  W   E        ♦ 8 6 2
  ♣ Q 3           S          ♣ K 10 9 7
              ♠ A Q 10 6 5
              ♥ 7 2
              ♦ K 9 3
              ♣ A 5 4
```

If you carelessly follow with the ♣3 on declarer's ace, he will draw trumps and eliminate the red suits. He will then exit with a second round of clubs to your queen. You will have to return a heart or a diamond, giving a ruff-and-sluff. Declarer will ruff in the dummy and throw the last club from his hand. (Partner cannot overtake your ♣Q with the ♣K because this would set up dummy's ♣J.)

Suppose you do find the best play of throwing your ♣Q on declarer's ace. The slam will then go down. When declarer plays a second round of clubs your partner can score two tricks in the suit.

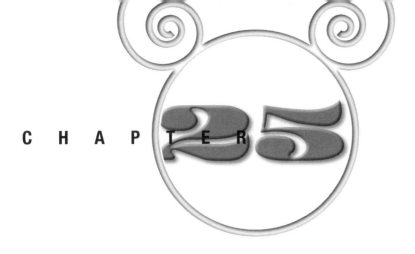

CHAPTER 25

DON'T RUFF PARTNER'S WINNER

 When your partner makes what appears to be an unusual play, do not condemn it, but ask yourself why the play was made.
J.B. Elwell

What is one of the most embarrassing gaffes you can perform when defending? Right! Ruffing partner's winner. You may be surprised to hear that there are occasions when you must steel yourself to perform this dastardly deed. Can you think of any yourself?

Ruffing partner's winner to attack a new suit

One reason may be that you wish to gain the lead to play another suit from the right side of the table. Take the East cards here:

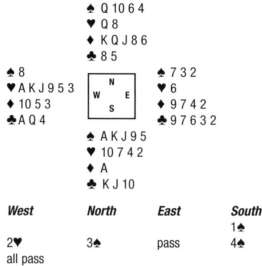

        ♠ Q 10 6 4
        ♥ Q 8
        ♦ K Q J 8 6
        ♣ 8 5

West	North	East	South
			1♠
2♥	3♠	pass	4♠
all pass			

Your spirits sink as you pick up those East cards. Fear not! Stay awake and you will be able to pick up a plus score. Partner leads the king of hearts and continues with the ace. What is your most helpful reaction?

There is only one good answer. You should ruff partner's ace of hearts and switch to a club. On the layout shown in the diagram partner will score two club tricks with his ace-queen and the contract will be beaten. If you fail to ruff, partner will be left on lead. He cannot attack clubs successfully from his side of the table and it will be an easy matter for declarer to draw trumps and discard his club losers on dummy's diamond suit.

There are other situations in which it would pay you to ruff partner's ♥A on that last deal. Suppose that your partner held the ♦A and the ♣K. Again it would be necessary for you to ruff at Trick 2 and switch to a club. This would be the only way to set up a club trick before declarer established the diamonds.

Ruffing a winner to save partner a guess

On the next deal you ruff partner's winner for a different reason — because if you leave him on lead he may not know what to do next.

```
                        ♠ K 6
                        ♥ K J 10 2
                        ♦ J 8 2
                        ♣ K Q J 7
    ♠ 4                ┌─────────┐      ♠ 8 7 3 2
    ♥ 7 4 3            │    N    │      ♥ 9 8 6
    ♦ A K Q 7 3        │ W     E │      ♦ 9 6
    ♣10 8 6 5          │    S    │      ♣ A 4 3 2
                       └─────────┘
                        ♠ A Q J 10 9 5
                        ♥ A Q 5
                        ♦ 10 5 4
                        ♣ 9
```

West	North	East	South
	1♣	pass	1♠
pass	1NT	pass	4♠
all pass			

Partner launches the defense with the king and ace of diamonds and, sitting East, you play high-low to show your doubleton. What are your thoughts when partner continues with the queen of diamonds? First of all, you expect declarer to follow to this trick, since partner would surely have overcalled 2♦ with six good diamonds. Secondly, you want partner to switch to a club after he has scored his three diamond tricks. How can you persuade him to do this?

Suppose you throw the ♣4, hoping that partner will read this as an encouraging discard (if that is your method). It's not a very high card, is it? Partner may not read your intentions. Similarly, you might throw the six of hearts, hoping that partner will read this as a discouraging card. It's not particularly low and partner may get it wrong. There is absolutely no need to take any risk in this position! You should ruff the third heart and cash the ace of clubs yourself. When you know what is best for the defense, take control and perform the necessary action yourself.

Ruffing partner's winner to promote a trump trick

There is another fairly common situation where you may choose to ruff partner's winner. You may be able to promote a trump trick. Take the East cards on this deal:

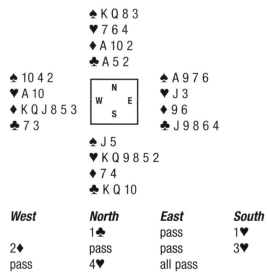

♠ K Q 8 3
♥ 7 6 4
♦ A 10 2
♣ A 5 2

♠ 10 4 2
♥ A 10
♦ K Q J 8 5 3
♣ 7 3

♠ A 9 7 6
♥ J 3
♦ 9 6
♣ J 9 8 6 4

♠ J 5
♥ K Q 9 8 5 2
♦ 7 4
♣ K Q 10

West	North	East	South
	1♣	pass	1♥
2♦	pass	pass	3♥
pass	4♥	all pass	

Partner starts with the ♦K and declarer wins with dummy's ace. When a trump is led to the king, your partner wins with the ace and cashes the ♦Q successfully. At Trick 4 he continues with the ♦J. What now?

You should ruff partner's diamond winner with the jack of trumps. Declarer overruffs with the queen and your partner's ♥10 is promoted. The defenders will now score one spade, two trumps and a diamond. One down!

'If partner held only five diamonds, his jack of diamonds might have scored a trick,' you may be thinking. That's true but the contract would still go one down if you ruffed the third diamond. Declarer would follow suit and you would cash the setting trick in spades. In any case, it was very likely that partner would hold six diamonds for his overcall at the two-level.

Summary

✓ It is normally a poor idea (to put it mildly!) to ruff your partner's winner. You should do so only when you have a specific purpose in mind.

✓ One such purpose is that a second suit may need to be attacked from your side of the table. You may need to lead through declarer's king or an ace-queen tenace.

✓ Another time to ruff partner's winner is when you know what further trick(s) can be cashed and partner may not.

✓ Ruffing a winner with your highest trump may promote a trump trick for partner.

DON'T RUFF PARTNER'S WINNER

NOW TRY THESE...

1)

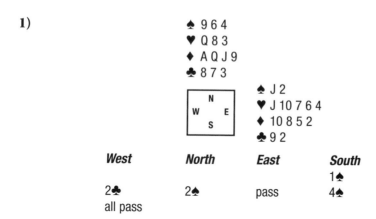

♠ 9 6 4
♥ Q 8 3
♦ A Q J 9
♣ 8 7 3

♠ J 2
♥ J 10 7 6 4
♦ 10 8 5 2
♣ 9 2

West	North	East	South
			1♠
2♣	2♠	pass	4♠
all pass			

Your partner leads the king and ace of clubs. You signal your doubleton by playing the nine and the two, and declarer follows with the four and the ten. Your partner then continues with the queen of clubs. Should you ruff or not? What is the reason for your choice?

2)

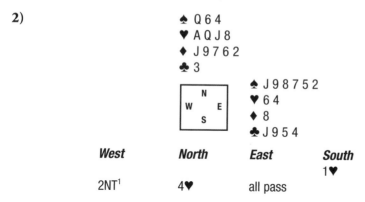

♠ Q 6 4
♥ A Q J 8
♦ J 9 7 6 2
♣ 3

♠ J 9 8 7 5 2
♥ 6 4
♦ 8
♣ J 9 5 4

West	North	East	South
			1♥
2NT[1]	4♥	all pass	

1   Unusual Notrump, showing at least 5-5 in the minors.

Partner leads the ♠A and continues with the ♦A, South dropping the ♦10. At Trick 3 partner leads the ♦K. Will you ruff the second round or not? What is the reason for your decision?

ANSWERS

1   You **should not** ruff. Your partner knows whether declarer has another club and you do not. It is up to him, therefore, to tell you what to do.

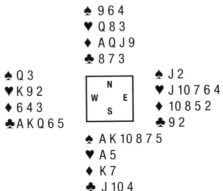

                          ♠ 9 6 4
                          ♥ Q 8 3
                          ♦ A Q J 9
                          ♣ 8 7 3

♠ Q 3   ♠ J 2
♥ K 9 2   ♥ J 10 7 6 4
♦ 6 4 3   ♦ 10 8 5 2
♣ A K Q 6 5   ♣ 9 2

                          ♠ A K 10 8 7 5
                          ♥ A 5
                          ♦ K 7
                          ♣ J 10 4

The winning defense is for West to cash three clubs and to play a fourth club. You ruff with the jack, promoting partner's queen of trumps.

If partner's hand were: ♠ Q 3 ♥ A 9 2 ♦ 6 4 ♣ A K Q J 6 5, he would cash the ♥A at Trick 3 and then play a low club, rather than a club winner. This would make it clear that you should ruff the third club.

2   You **should** ruff the second diamond and give partner a spade ruff. Partner surely has a singleton ♠A. With A-x, he would have cashed a top diamond first, keeping a spade switch in reserve. The cards lie like this:

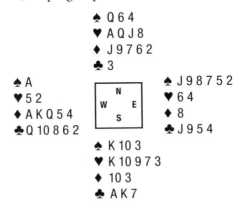

                          ♠ Q 6 4
                          ♥ A Q J 8
                          ♦ J 9 7 6 2
                          ♣ 3

♠ A   ♠ J 9 8 7 5 2
♥ 5 2   ♥ 6 4
♦ A K Q 5 4   ♦ 8
♣ Q 10 8 6 2   ♣ J 9 5 4

                          ♠ K 10 3
                          ♥ K 10 9 7 3
                          ♦ 10 3
                          ♣ A K 7

Note South's deceptive ♦10 on the first round, making your ♦8 look like the first half of a doubleton. That is why partner could not afford to lead a low diamond at Trick 3, forcing you to ruff the trick.

ABTA Book of the Year Award Winners

25 Bridge Conventions You Should Know
by Barbara Seagram and Marc Smith
(foreword by Eddie Kantar)
192pp., PB   Can $19.95   US$ 15.95

Eddie Kantar teaches Modern Bridge Defense
Eddie Kantar teaches Advanced Bridge Defense
by Eddie Kantar
each 240pp., PB   Can $27.95   US$ 19.95

Also available in Interactive CD-ROM Editions
Modern Bridge Defense   Can $69.95   US$ 49.95
Advanced Bridge Defense Can $69.95   US$ 49.95

The Bridge Technique Series
by David Bird & Marc Smith
each 64pp. PB   Can $7.95   US $5.95

Deceptive Card Play	Planning in Suit Contracts
Defensive Signaling	Reading the Cards
Eliminations and Throw-Ins	Safety Plays
Entry Management	Squeezes for Everyone
Planning in Defense	Tricks with Finesses
Planning in Notrump Contracts	Tricks with Trumps

Around the World in 80 Hands by Zia Mahmood with David Burn
256pp., PB   Can $22.95   US $16.95

A Study in Silver *A second collection of bridge stories* by David Silver
128pp., PB   Can $12.95   US $9.95

Becoming a Bridge Expert by Frank Stewart
300pp., PB   Can $27.95   US $19.95

Best of Bridge Today Digest by Matthew and Pamela Granovetter
192pp., PB   Can $19.95   US $14.95

Bridge Problems for a New Millennium by Julian Pottage
160pp., PB   Can $14.95   US $11.95

Bridge the Silver Way by David Silver and Tim Bourke
192pp., PB   Can $19.95   US $14.95

Bridge Squeezes for Everyone* *Yes, even you!* by David Bird
220pp., PB   Can $24.95   US $17.95

Bridge: 25 Steps to Learning 2/1
by Paul Thurston (foreword by Eric Kokish)
192pp., PB   Can $19.95   US $15.95

Bridge: 25 Ways to Compete in the Bidding.
by Barbara Seagram and Marc Smith
220pp., PB   Can $19.95   US $15.95

Bridge, Zia... and me by Michael Rosenberg
(foreword by Zia Mahmood)
192pp., PB   Can $19.95   US $15.95

Challenge Your Declarer Play by Danny Roth
128pp., PB   Can $12.95   US $ 9.95

Classic Kantar   a collection of bridge humor by Eddie Kantar
192pp., PB   Can $19.95   US $14.95

Competitive Bidding in the 21st Century by Marshall Miles
254pp., PB   Can $22.95   US. $16.95

Countdown to Winning Bridge by Tim Bourke and Marc Smith
192pp., PB   Can $19.95   US $15.95

Eddie Kantar teaches Topics in Declarer Play at Bridge
by Eddie Kantar
240 pp., PB   Can $27.95   US $19.95

For Love or Money *The Life of a Bridge Journalist*
by Mark Horton and Brian Senior
189pp., PB   Can $22.95   US $16.95

Focus On Declarer Play by Danny Roth
128pp., PB   Can $12.95   US $9.95